THE END OF SETTLEMENT

The End of Settlement

why the 2023 referendum failed

Damien Freeman

Connor Court Publishing

The End of Settlement: why the 2023 referendum failed

Damien Freeman

Published in 2024 by Connor Court Publishing Pty Ltd

Connor Court Publishing Pty Ltd
PO Box 7257
Redland Bay QLD 4165
sales@connorcourt.com
www.connorcourt.com

Printed in Australia

ISBN: 9781923224094

Front Cover: Ian James

Contents

Acknowledgements

I am grateful to Associate Professor Richard Colledge, executive dean of theology and philosophy, for enabling me to be appointed an Honorary Fellow of Australian Catholic University shortly before I embarked on this project, as I am to Dallas McInerney, chief executive officer of Catholic Schools NSW, for naming me a research fellow of the Kathleen Burrow Research Institute, and to Georgina Downer, chief executive officer, for naming me a Fellow of the Robert Menzies Institute at the University of Melbourne whilst I was working on the manuscript.

This book draws together different parts of my thinking over the last decade, particularly my work in seeking to find a settlement through which Aboriginal and Torres Strait Islander peoples might be recognised in the Australian Constitution. This was a journey that I began with Julian Leeser MP before he entered parliament. He continued to show great leadership after entering parliament, when I continued my work with Uphold & Recognise, the non-profit organisation that we set up together. I am grateful to him for his leadership, as I am to Noel Pearson at Cape York Institute, Associate Professor Shireen Morris at Macquarie University, Emeritus Professor Greg Craven AO at Australian Catholic University, and Professor Emerita Anne Twomey AO at the University of Sydney, who worked with us at the initial stage. At Uphold & Recognise, I am especially grateful for the leadership shown by our chairman, Sean Gordon AM, and the encouragement of our fellow directors, the Honourable Ken Wyatt AM, Associate

Professor Michael Reynolds, Ian McGill, Sam Fay, Theresa Ardler, and our executive director, Kerry Pinkstone.

The manuscript for this book has benefited from the attention that a number of kind readers have paid to it. I am grateful for different critical perspectives provided by the Reverend Peter Kurti, Dr Michael Easson AM, Professor Brenton Prosser, Kerry Pinkstone, and one reader who wishes to remain nameless but is known unto God.

Finally, I am grateful to Professor Bryan Turner for his intellectual companionship and for inviting me to work on a project funded by the Menzies Australia Institute at King's College London whilst I was simultaneously working on this book.

DTF

1

Settlement Politics

"It was never as warm and cuddly as that," John Howard writes in *A Sense of Balance* when reflecting on the way in which "some commentators nostalgically refer to the 1980s as a golden era when the major parties came together to implement good policy." Although we should be wary of nostalgia, Howard never doubts that there were "key instances when the major parties managed to agree." Remembering this is all the more important today because, as Howard also reminds us, "there is no evidence of bipartisanship in Australian politics now."

To avoid the nostalgia is to understand the sense in which opponents came together; the sense in which they managed to agree. It wasn't the case that differences dissolved. Concurrence took a particular form; a form that admitted of ongoing disagreement even in the face of agreement about the need to implement fundamental policy reforms. Such concurrence might be called *settlement politics*.

'Settlement' can mean many things, but the relevant sense is a compromise through which parties voluntarily end a dispute. Settlement politics is the activity of reaching political agreement through a form of compromise. Settlement politics has been central to Australian political history. But is settlement politics still possible? If the 2023 referendum is anything to go by, then it seems like there is no hope for settlement politics in Australia anymore. If that is the case, then what is the way forward? How are we to navigate our political future when it comes to major change? And, if settlement politics is critical for achieving certain forms of major reform, such as constitutional amendment, are we best advised to give up on any attempt at such major reform in the near future?

These questions are important ones, and this book lays out one way of approaching them. It begins with a discussion of Paul Kelly's account of the Australian Settlement in *The End of Certainty*. According to Kelly, the first eighty years of the Commonwealth were dominated by the settlement established by Alfred Deakin. This provided a shared set of ideas that were broadly accepted across the political divides. These ideas were challenged and abandoned in the 1980s, when, he argues, a new basis for public policy was required. The undoing of the Australian Settlement was largely the work of Bob Hawke and Paul Keating as prime minister and treasurer. In doing so, they found support in the shadow treasurer, John Howard, who had independently reached similar conclusions about the necessity of reform.

The emphasis of Kelly's account is how a set of propositions about Australia's governance was abandoned and replaced, and the sense in which this undermined the certainty that had hitherto prevailed in Australian politics. A subtheme in his account, which deserves more attention, is the political concurrence that attended the dismantling of the Australian Settlement and the construction of a replacement for it. Although an agreed set of principles was abandoned, there was broad agreement about the need to abandon them and what should replace them. The first chapter of this book is concerned with the sense in which there was agreement about what needed to be done and how to do it. Such agreement is an example of settlement politics. Politicians across the political divides found agreement about how to go about implementing reform, even if they were still conscious of their other political disagreements.

If settlement politics has been a dominant feature of Australian politics in the twentieth century, what exactly is it and why might it be a good thing? The second chapter draws on the reflections of Sir Roger Scruton to build up an account of what settlement politics is. This account comes from Scruton's understanding of the Church of England as a settlement. The religious and political conflict of sixteenth-century England fed into a civil war in the seventeenth century, the abolition of the monarchy and its restoration, and further instability. When stability was finally achieved with the Glorious Revolution in 1688, the religious conflict did not end with a victory for one side, so much as an accommodation of difference. It was a religious settlement that could be traced back to Elizabeth I. It relied on a sense of ambiguity to identify enough commonality that profound theological differences could coexist peacefully within a single polity. This was a settlement that Scruton claims endured and served England well for three centuries, until changes in the late twentieth century meant it was no longer fit for purpose.

When we understand the sense in which the Church of England developed as a settlement, we get a better sense of what settlement politics is. It is not a matter of consensus in the sense that everyone agrees about everything. It is not a matter of synthesising the alternative perspectives, so that we arrive at an approach that incorporates enough of each of the rival perspectives. Rather, it is a matter of finding a way forward that draws on ambiguity to allow different perspectives to provide their own way of justifying the arrangements, even if there is still profound disagreement between them. This sense of settlement politics can be seen to underpin both the Australian Settlement and its undoing. It has been an important feature of Australian politics for a long time, but a feature that may no longer be possible to sustain.

In the period since the end of certainty, John Howard has been one of the most dominant political figures. His premiership was the longest in the post-Australian Settlement era. The third chapter considers him in relation to settlement politics. There are three senses in which he is relevant to this discussion. First, he was a major player when the Australian Settlement was being dismantled in the 1980s by Hawke and Keating, and his role as shadow treasurer enabled this major reform to occur in an uncontentious way. Secondly, as leader of the Liberal Party, and as its elder statesman, he frequently articulated his vision of the party as itself a kind of settlement that allowed conservatism and liberalism to co-exist. Finally, as the title of his book, *A Sense of Balance*, suggests, he sees Australian society as a kind of settlement in which competing approaches can co-exist.

If we accept that Howard is a settlement politician, what is the relevance of his settlement politics today? Is it desirable to engage in settlement politics, and, if so, is it still possible? The fifth chapter considers changes that might mean it is no longer relevant. The 2023 Edelman Trust Barometer paints a picture of an Australia in which trust is decreasing and polarisation is increasing. These changes have consequences for politics. In an increasingly polarised society, it seems settlement politics is ever more difficult. Yet it might also be argued that as politicians abandon settlement politics, polarisation is likely to increase. If settlement politics is desirable, then we need to get clear about its relationship with trust and polarisation in order to understand whether we should be trying to pursue settlement politics in an increasingly polarised Australia, and, if so, how we go about doing it.

This is not merely a speculative discussion. It culminates in an analysis of the 2023 referendum. In the sixth chapter, the genesis of the referendum proposal is shown to have been a settlement project that aimed to find common ground between advocates for constitutional recognition of Aboriginal and Torres Strait Islander peoples and conservative critics of their initial proposal for achieving this. By working together, they believed that they hit upon a settlement that could achieve the concurrence necessary for a successful referendum to alter the Australian Constitution.

The seventh chapter discusses how this settlement project failed. When the bill for a constitution alteration was being negotiated, and when the referendum campaign began after the bill passed both houses of parliament, what it revealed was a polarised society that made a successful referendum impossible. This failure raises many questions. For present purposes, the most pertinent are those relating to settlement politics.

Does the failure of the referendum mean that settlement politics is no longer possible? As the book shows, settlement politics has served England and Australia well over the centuries. It continues to have much to commend it as we face future political challenges. For settlement politics to be effective, however, politicians need to be willing and able to engage with one another and their challenges in a certain way. Yet for this to happen, the right circumstances are also necessary. Yes, rivals need to see the need to settle their differences, but they also need to see a pathway to settlement. Once that moment passes, we are in the realm of goodwill rather than settlement politics.

No good comes of adopting a utopian attitude to the future of Australian politics. Indeed, this is even more dangerous than adopting a nostalgic attitude to its history. A proper understanding of how politicians have worked effectively in the past might provide insights for how they could work effectively in the future. If it turns out that the future is going to be so very different from the past, it may be that a different kind of politics is required. Even so, it is important to understand what has worked in the past and what we might have to give up when confronting future challenges. For all these reasons, it's worth taking the time to think carefully about settlement politics.

2

Ending the Australian Settlement

The Big Picture was the nickname given to Tom Roberts's 10 x 17-foot painting of the Duke of Cornwall and York opening the first Australian Parliament on behalf of King Edward VII in 1901. It was so called because of its size, and it captures the mood that attended the opening of the first parliament as well as depicting some of the multitude who were present. But there is a difference between the big picture of the dignified state occasion that was the opening of parliament and the big picture of the grubbier business that is the politics that played out in this new institution.

When it comes to understanding the big picture of Australian politics in the twentieth century, Paul Kelly maintains that there were two critical points of inflection: the development of the *Australian Settlement* by Australia's second prime minister, Alfred Deakin, in the first decade of the federation, and the dismantling of this settlement by Bob Hawke and Paul Keating eighty years later. One set of settled policies was replaced by another set of quite different policies. Both represented a position acceptable to politicians across political divides who remained in profound disagreement, even though they were able to support these policies. This peculiar form of convergence in the midst of disagreement was a feature of Australian political history throughout the first century of Australian federation, but one that would not last into the second century.

Deakin's settlement

Kelly was not the first person to identify this development. What he describes as the Australian Settlement had been identified at least as early as 1930 by Sir Keith Hancock as the settled policy of the country. This consisted of five policies: in immigration, the White Australia policy; in commerce, protectionism; in industrial relations, centralised wage arbitration; in social policy, state paternalism; and in defence and international relations, imperial benevolence. These were the policies established by Deakin in the first decade of the federation, and they became policies about which there was broad agreement.

To understand how the Australian Settlement took shape is to understand how people with a range of different political perspectives arrived at the conclusion that they should support these policies. Before Federation, one of the biggest political divides was between the protectionists and the free traders. The colony of Victoria was protectionist and imposed tariffs on imports from other colonies and beyond. The colony of New South Wales had a policy of free trade and did not impose tariffs. The free traders had a victory in the drafting of the Australian Constitution, which stipulated that trade between the new states of the Commonwealth must be absolutely free. What remained to be decided by the new Commonwealth Parliament, however, was whether tariffs should be imposed on imports from overseas.

Gradually, a system of tariffs was introduced to protect local industries that could not do battle with foreign competitors. This was because some politicians wanted to protect inefficient manufacturers. Others, like Deakin, realised that this was not entirely desirable, but saw that their own political interest lay in promoting protectionism. Besides, in Victoria, where there was a sizable manufacturing industry, public sentiment was overwhelmingly in favour of protectionism. Hence, Deakin became a protectionist of convenience, and in time the leader of the Protectionist Party.

Whilst it is obvious why the Protectionist Party would support protectionism, it is less obvious why the Labor Party would support it. To understand this, one needs to appreciate that the policy of centralised wage arbitration was tied to protectionism. The Commonwealth Conciliation and Arbitration Act created a system of conciliation and arbitration through which a fair and reasonable award wage could be established. It did more than that, however, as it also imposed a legal obligation on protected industrialists to share the bounty of protectionism by paying their employees fair and reasonable wages as determined by the award. In this way, centralised wage arbitration was inextricably linked to protectionism in what became known as *New Protectionism*. By forcing industrialists to pay fair and reasonable wages on pain of losing the benefits of the tariff that protected them, a commercial imperative for paying a fair and reasonable wage was created. This gave the Labor Party a reason to support New Protectionism: the wages of the working classes would be secured. Indeed, whenever they could, Labor parliamentarians propped up Deakin's Protectionists in the first decade after Federation.

In the first decade of the new parliament, there were three main parties who were roughly equal in strength: the Protectionists, the Free Traders, and Labor. Two of those three parties now had a reason to support New Protectionism, but what about the third? The whole point of the Free Trade Party was to oppose protectionism. The Free Traders found themselves in a difficult position. Although they opposed the Protectionists' position on tariffs, they also opposed Labor's socialism. So they had a choice: either join with the Protectionists to create an anti-Labor party, or risk being politically marginalised and allowing Labor to prevail. The need to oppose socialism was such that they were prepared to tolerate New Protectionism and join forces with the Protectionists in 1909 to create the Commonwealth Liberal Party, in what became known as the Fusion. A two-party system was now established, and it was based on Labor vs anti-Labor, rather than on protectionism vs free trade, which had dominated colonial politics.

The Commonwealth Liberal Party combined Deakin's Protectionists and Reid's anti-socialist Free Traders, who had common cause in being anti-socialist. Although this party did not last, after splitting in 1929, liberals and conservatives would finally reunite under Robert Menzies in 1944 to form the Liberal Party of Australia. The other important anti-Labor party emerged in 1920 in the form of the Country Party. This party represented the primary producers who were significantly disadvantaged by protectionism as they relied on exporting their produce. New Protectionism did not benefit them in the way that it did the industrialists and the workers. And yet even the Country Party was prepared to support New Protectionism, on condition that it secured compensation for the primary producers.

At this point, one starts to see how New Protectionism delivered prosperity for everyone and this created a further justification for the policy. This is what Kelly calls the conservative 'sentimental traditionalist' position: New Protectionism had become the Australian way, and conservatives felt committed to upholding the settled policies that provided the prosperity that underpinned the Australian way of life. This position was exemplified by Malcolm Fraser's economic policy, and would remain the Liberal Party position until challenged by Howard.

Protectionism and wage arbitration were only two of Deakin's five settled policies. By focusing on them, however, we can get a sense of how people with a range of different political perspectives converged on policies that most of them would not particularly have otherwise liked. Industrialists, workers, farmers, anti-socialist liberals, and conservatives each ended up with their own reason for supporting these policies despite their different reservations about the policies.

Critiques of settlement policies

The fact of this political convergence does not detract from the fact that these policies had their critics. Throughout the entire period of the Australian Settlement, criticism of settlement policies was in the public domain. George Reid had served as premier of New South Wales before entering the first Commonwealth Parliament in 1901. He had consistently argued against protectionism since 1875, drawing on Adam Smith and the nineteenth-century English politician and free-trade campaigner, Richard Cobden, to make the case for why protectionism was wrong as a matter of principle.

Protectionism was introduced, however, and by 1930 it was clear that protectionism was not working from Edward Shann's *Economic History of Australia* and Sir Keith Hancock's *Australia*, which both demonstrated that protection of one industry came at a cost to another industry, which then required compensation. In 1964, Donald Horne expressed contempt for the failure of Australian leaders to step up to the real challenges in *The Lucky Country*. By the dying days of the Fraser government, there was renewed interest in this line of critique amongst the Crossroads group. Crossroads was formed in 1980 with Liberal parliamentarians and others outside parliament who were interested in developing a libertarian critique. This drew on Adam Smith, but also on the more recent work of Milton Friedman and Friedrich Hayek to explain why the status quo was not working, and to develop a free-market alternative.

Labor and economic deregulation

Despite the longstanding awareness that the settlement policies were problematic, the political commitment endured until the 1980s because too many people had too many reasons to remain committed despite awareness of the problems. In *The End of Certainty*, Kelly tells the story of the politics of the 1980s as the undoing of the Australian Settlement and its replacement with alternative policies. Some of this had gotten underway earlier, notably Harold Holt had begun the process of dismantling the White Australia policy which was completed by Gough Whitlam, before Fraser started talking about multiculturalism as a replacement policy. It was particularly in the realm of economic policy that hard changes had to be made; changes that moved towards a free-market economy.

Kelly presents the floating of the Australian dollar and the deregulation of the financial system as the two most influential economic decisions of the decade. The dollar was floated on 9 December 1983, yet in mid-1983 the Labor government was still opposed to surrendering the federal government's control of key aspects of the economy. The previous government had commissioned a committee chaired by Sir Keith Campbell, whose 1981 report recommended deregulation, however, this was rejected by the Labor opposition. Yet, in a very short space of time, Hawke and Keating both came to understand that market forces, rather than official intervention, would be the best way of achieving a more efficient economy. This was a response to changing economic circumstances. In the decade 1973-1983, the Australian economy, along with those of other countries, was becoming part of an integrated global market. It was apparent by 1983 that it was no longer sustainable for government officials to manage an official exchange rate for the dollar. Although it ran counter to Labor policy, Hawke and Keating had both independently come to the conclusion that deregulation was inevitable. The decision to float the dollar was a pragmatic response to a capital inflow crisis in October 1983, and then a worse crisis in December. The decision was driven by the need to respond to circumstances in which the existing system had failed. It was not driven by ideological zeal. In the financial markets of the 1980s, government intervention was far less effective. A monetary crisis had prompted the decision to float the dollar, but not provided the solution. As Kelly explains, Hawke and Keating came to accept that markets were the solution to economic problems, and with this acceptance followed the decisions to deregulate the financial markets and entry of foreign banks in 1984.

These reforms did not come easy to Labor. There was the expected backlash that the Hawke administration was abandoning Labor's aspiration of taming capital. The Labor government was instead presenting itself as a government of economic management which had cordial relations with a new generation of businessmen. The challenge was to explain how a social democratic party could support free-market reforms. Hawke prepared the way for this in his Curtin Lecture in September 1983, when he said, "Social Democrats have no reason to deny the capacity of markets to allocate resources efficiently . . . I see no virtue in regulation of economic activity for its own sake and I believe that where markets are working effectively they should be left to do their job."

Liberals and economic deregulation

As Kelly tells the story, an important feature of how these reforms came about is that the Labor government did not meet with resistance from the conservative opposition. Indeed, as shadow treasurer, John Howard was a keen supporter of reforms that moved Australia towards a free-market economy. It may be difficult for the contemporary Liberal Party to acknowledge this, but the party had not always been wedded to market economics. From Menzies to Fraser, there was a real commitment to upholding the Australian tradition when it came to economic policy, and that meant a large role for the government in controlling all aspects of the economy.

For decades, the sole advocate for market economics in the federal parliament was C. R. 'Bert' Kelly, who served as the Liberal member for Wakefield from 1958 until 1977. On 19 January 1997, the prime minister, John Howard, issued a statement on Kelly's death. He said, "Bert Kelly was almost certainly the first and definitely the foremost parliamentary advocate in the post World War II period of lower tariffs and freer trade." He noted that Kelly advocated for free-market reforms "at a time when it was unfashionable to do so." His conclusion is a reminder of how dramatically political attitudes had changed in the twenty years since Kelly left parliament: "Those now on the Australian political scene who take it as a given that the contemporary economic debate is largely about the pace of further change, not whether we should return to the days of high protection, should remember the immense debt of gratitude which is owed to Bert Kelly." It was Kelly's disciples who would become the dries within the federal Liberal Party and ultimately change the party's philosophy.

In the United Kingdom, Margaret Thatcher's supporters took to describing those in the Conservative Party who opposed her policies as 'wet'. In return, her opponents described her supporters as being 'dry'. The distinction between wets and dries was then imported into Australia, where those advocating radical economic reform were labelled 'dries' and those who remained committed to upholding the economic policy of the Australian Settlement, 'wets'. The difference between the British and Australian situations was that in Britain the dries were those who supported the leader's policy whereas in Australia the dries were those who advocated change from the existing party policy.

The dry campaign began in 1980 when a West Australian Liberal MP, John Hyde, publicly criticised the economic policy that Fraser espoused; a policy position that was broadly consistent with that of Menzies. The problem was that the international economic circumstances had changed so much that a position that had seemed plausible in Menzies's day was no longer plausible in Fraser's day. Hyde worked closely with Peter Shack, Jim Carlton, and Murray Sainsbury to establish a network of likeminded Liberals who saw the need for radical economic reform. They formed the Crossroads group, which had its first conference in Sydney in 1981. The Crossroads Conference members became the counter-establishment voice in conservative politics, advocating radical economic reform that would see Australia transition to a market economy with minimal government intervention.

The dries were pragmatic people who could see that changed circumstances demanded changed policies, but they were also ideologically motivated. They were impressed by the new ideological stance of libertarianism that had been espoused in the economics of Margaret Thatcher in the United Kingdom and Ronald Reagan in the United States. They proposed that the Liberal Party should embrace a similar policy of free-market economics. Their new philosophy drew on Adam Smith, Milton Friedman, and Friedrich Hayek. From Smith's *Wealth of Nations*, they took the idea that the public interest is served best by enabling private individuals to transact business in a way that serves their own interests. From Friedman, they took the argument that government intervention in a country's economy was the cause of economic problems rather than the cure for them (a repudiation of the highly influential economist, John Maynard Keynes). From Hayek, they took their understanding of the proper function of government: restoring and expanding the freedom of the individual. This libertarian ideology was not merely a policy response to the economic challenges the country faced. It was a re-envisaging of the philosophical purpose of the Liberal Party.

Fraser remained faithful to the old mission of the Liberal Party as protector of the economic status quo. As such, he rejected the push from the dries to change the party's ideology, which he regarded as "too impractical and too puritanical." His treasurer, Howard, had, however, become identified as one of the leading dries, and saw the need for change. The change involved a fundamental shift in the party's understanding of itself which the wets resisted. There was protracted fighting within the party, however, the wets could not develop any viable alternative to the dries' market-based solutions. In the end, they capitulated after Fraser's defeat. As treasurer, Howard, who came to be seen as a leading economic radical, was hampered by an economically conservative prime minister. He was strongly identified with the push to change Liberal Party policy to embrace the free market, and this ultimately prevailed when the party policy changed. The Liberal Federal Council adopted the dries' free-market ideology at a meeting in October 1983, and, after the shadow ministry and coalition parties formally approved the change, the principles were announced as Liberal Party policy on 12 April 1984.

When economic reform came under Hawke and Keating, it was a realisation of what Howard had seen needed to happen, but which was frustrated by Fraser who could not see it. So, rather than resisting change, as shadow treasurer he supported the government's reforms but criticised them for not going far enough. When Doug Anthony told Howard that he proposed to make a statement denouncing the float of the dollar as a policy that was not in the national interest, Kelly records Howard's response to Anthony: "If you say that, I'll have no option but to repudiate your position as shadow treasurer." Kelly adds the gloss: "They argued, then Anthony relented. A short time later he left politics." That captures the nature of Howard's support for Keating's announcement. He was not about to praise his opponent, but nor was he going to allow the perception that the opposition rejected a policy that he knew to be correct. It also captures the nature of the wets' capitulation to Howard.

Parties converge for new settlement

Australia had moved from one set of settled policies to a very different set. Kelly gives full credit to the Labor Party for this, although he also acknowledges its limitations. Whilst Hawke felt free enough from vested financial interests to deregulate the financial system, the Labor Party's ties to the unions meant that it was unable to deregulate the labour market. Kelly concludes, "The moral, perhaps, is that Labor was more ruthless in discarding old habits with business and finance while the Liberals could be more ruthless with the unions." It was also a matter of Labor seizing opportunities where they existed. Kelly points out that planning for financial deregulation had progressed significantly under the Liberal government, whereas there had been no planning for labour market deregulation. Moreover, the monetary crisis in 1983 presented an opportunity where there was no similar opportunity for labour deregulation. That said, Labor remained committed to centralised wage-fixing. Howard, in opposition, had identified two aims in industrial relations reform: to reduce union power and to adopt a system for wages that reflected market forces. Labor would concede some ground here by acknowledging the need for an enterprise bargaining system. This part of the Australian Settlement would have to wait and be dismantled by the Liberals, but Labor had signalled that it understood this would have to go—there may not have been consensus, but there was ever more convergence.

The story that Kelly presents of Labor and Liberal convergence on economic reform is not a story of a joint activity or compromise. It is a matter of two separate journeys that arrive at the same point. In particular, it is not an instance of what Hawke was fond of calling *consensus*. Consensus was Hawke's instrument of industrial relations. He was able to manage wage growth through the Accord, which brought unions and business together. Hawke achieved substantive agreement about wages between these parties. Such consensus is a co-operative activity. It would be a mistake to think that the story of the 1980s is the story of Liberal and Labor consensus in this sense. Rather, it was a matter of a Labor government realising that the changing international economics demanded pragmatic policy responses which meant accepting that old hostilities to the free market had to be consigned to history, and a Liberal opposition fundamentally redeveloping its philosophy from being the upholders of an economic settlement to being libertarian economic radicals. As Kelly explains, these were two quite different political journeys that arrived at the same point.

The disagreement on the right was the challenge that the radical liberals posed to the sentimental traditionalists. The radicals had embraced the libertarian ideology which was completely at odds with the Liberal Party's conception of itself as the upholders of the Australian tradition that had been threatened by the excesses of the Whitlam years but restored in the Fraser years. The radicals, led by Howard, succeeded in completely changing the economic philosophy of their party – albeit at considerable cost. As Kelly writes, "But the radical liberals had not fully grasped the consequences of their challenge. They were striking at the power structure of conservative Australia. Their success would come only with the overthrow of the old order – and that dictated a clash of arms."

The disagreement on the left was the challenge that embracing the free market posed to the Labor Party's mission – the Light on the Hill. Labor, if not strictly socialist, had nevertheless always remained committed to the idea that the purpose of achieving government was to be a guiding light for the betterment of society; to improve the lot of the downtrodden. This was directly challenged by Hawke and Keating's embrace of the free market, which drastically reimagined the capacity of any Labor government to be the Light on the Hill. As Kelly writes, "Throughout its existence the Labor Party had sought to improve or civilise the capitalist economy through the intervention of the state. Under Hawke and Keating it sought to improve the economy by unleashing the weapon of the market. This was a fundamental leap in Labor politics." For some, this was a betrayal of Labor's aspirations for the Light on the Hill; for others, this was the only way Labor could achieve social reform in a new age.

Although there were clearly competing Labor and Liberal agenda, what emerged was a situation in which the only way to pursue any of the competing agenda was to embrace reform. So, there was agreement about pushing ahead with reform, even if there remained disagreements about what different politicians sought to achieve for Australia as a society through the reform. Kelly writes that "the political story of the 1980s is how Labor and Liberal, once joint upholders of the old system, became joint architects of the new system." Kelly is rightly concerned with telling the story of the new system that came to replace the old one. There is a second strand to this story, however, and it should not be glossed over. It concerns the similarity between the way in which the old system had been upheld and the way in which a new system replaced the old. This is captured in Kelly's use of the word 'joint'. Labor and Liberal were *joint* upholders of the old system and *joint* architects of the new one.

Settlement politics in the 1980s

As the quote from Howard at the beginning of this book reminds us, it is easy to misunderstand the sense in which Labor and Liberal were joint upholders and joint architects. It was not "warm and cuddly." These joint activities involved maintaining disagreement in the midst of agreement. This is what we mean by *settlement politics*, which will be explained more thoroughly in the next chapter. For the time being, what matters is that, although two quite different approaches were taken in the first eighty years and the following decade, there is a similarity between the two. Each was an example of settlement politics.

In 1899, the French historian and geographer, Albert Métin, paid a visit to Australia to study social and economic development in the colonies. He had a personal interest in the study of Anglo-Saxon societies, and his research was also funded by the Third Republic, which was interested in gathering data about recent developments abroad. The visit resulted in the publication of a book in 1901, *Le socialisme sans doctrines*, or in translation, *Socialism without Doctrine*. The book contained his assessment of Australian public policy, which, he argued, saw the state adopt policies that achieved the objectives of socialism in labour and economic policy, but did so without acknowledging any socialist ideological objective. Many have come to appreciate the accuracy of his insight. This is indeed central to the Australian Settlement's policies of state paternalism, but also to the broad acceptance of these policies. The anti-socialist parties could never have accepted policies that were advanced as the realisation of socialism in Australia. They could accept the policies, however, if they were detached from socialist ideology.

When it came time for economic deregulation, something similar happened. Although the Liberal Party was ready to sign up to the economic libertarian ideology, the Labor Party was not. It was prepared to accept reforms that achieved economic deregulation out of necessity, but its own ideological commitments prevented it from signing up to the libertarian ideology. So what emerged as a replacement for the bipartisan commitment to socialism without doctrine might be described as *economic deregulation without doctrine*.

Australian exceptionalism in the 1990s

What happened to settlement politics after the 1980s? Kelly's narrative continues in *The March of Patriots*, the sequel to *The End of Certainty*, which covers the years 1991 to 2001. His

20

thesis is that, despite all their differences, Keating and Howard were essentially committed to the same project, which he calls *Australian Exceptionalism*. This was the idea that economic reform in Australia is a special case: "a transformation from the pre-1983 protected economy of the old Australian Settlement . . . faithful to Australian values of economic pragmatism, social egalitarianism and practical utility." It was *exceptional* because "it avoided the laissez-faire laxity of the American system and the stifling controls of the European system." Kelly argues that when the time came to replace the Australian Settlement's economic policies, the response was a combination of economic deregulation and a commitment to the 'fair go' – "an Australian-made synthesis of a decent society and a strong economy."

Kelly argues that the high point of neo-liberalism, or free-market ideological purity, was the *Fightback!* manifesto advocated by John Hewson as opposition leader in the 1993 election campaign. Hewson suffered a significant and unexpected defeat. After that, Kelly argues, the Liberals abandoned ideological purity in their policymaking. They saw that electoral success required them to temper free-market economics with an unambiguous commitment to the fair go. Thus, Kelly maintains, Howard's approach was continuous with Keating's in a way that Hewson's was not. This enables him to argue that Australian Exceptionalism was a bipartisan project: although the foundations were laid in the Hawke-Keating years, the project was continued by Howard when he was in government. It is true that the Liberal Party's embrace of free-market reforms was ideological whereas the Labor Party's was pragmatic. After the *Fightback!* fiasco, the Liberals' ideology remained neo-liberalism but their policymaking became Australian Exceptionalism – there was a disconnect between the ideology and the policymaking.

Rudd's take on Australian exceptionalism

The March of Patriots was launched by Kevin Rudd at Parliament House on 7 September 2009. The prime minister had launched Thomas Keneally's history of Australia a couple of weeks earlier. In launching Kelly's book, Rudd rejected the second of Kelly's two central claims. Although he accepted the idea that Australian Exceptionalism had replaced the Australian Settlement, he was adamant that this was not a bipartisan achievement as presented by Kelly. Rudd argued that this was a product of Labor policymaking, and that Howard's government had only watered it down. He advanced the case that the Liberals remained committed to neo-liberalism and that Kelly was wrong to claim that this ended with the defeat of Hewson and *Fightback!* The difficulty with Rudd's analysis is that it does not distinguish carefully enough between the ideology and the policymaking. Kelly's point is that Alexander Downer, Peter Costello, and Howard all understood that policymaking had to be Australian Exceptionalism rather than strictly neo-liberal if it was to be acceptable to the electorate.

The opposition leader, Malcolm Turnbull, was sitting behind Kelly at the launch and lent forward to whisper what he thought of Rudd's analysis. At a dinner to celebrate the centenary of the Fusion of the Protectionists and the Free Traders, Turnbull's response was louder. He told the assembled guests that "Kevin Rudd is treating the recent history of this nation as a political plaything; something to be manipulated – in the Orwellian style of the Big Lie." Rudd had said, "we would describe our opponents as indolent – perhaps not always opposing the great transformational reforms engineered by Labor during its 13 years in office, but barely adding to that reform agenda during their 12 years in office." Turnbull said Rudd's claims were "as audacious as they are mendacious." He acknowledged that both sides of politics had contributed to the economic and structural reforms, concluding, "We in the coalition are not so conceited to claim all the credit."

The March of Patriots launch is a reminder of how far Australian politics had moved from settlement politics by 2009. No longer was it even possible for a prime minister to launch a book that advanced the thesis that there had been bipartisanship in the previous decade without feeling the need to denounce that thesis. Australian politics had become polarised.

It wasn't that everyone agreed about everything in the 1980s. They didn't. There was bitter disagreement in some senses, but in other senses they were able to work together despite this. To understand how this was possible is to understand settlement politics. Once we have a grasp of this idea of settlement politics, we can consider how well it explains the politics of Australia in the twentieth century. Assuming that it has some explanatory power, the next question is whether settlement politics is still possible.

3

Starting the Anglican
Settlement

Writing in *Our Church: a personal history of the Church of England*, the British philosopher Sir Roger Scruton tells the story of religious conflict in sixteenth and seventeenth-century England. He also explains how the Church of England resolved the conflict: "gradually, as religious passions cooled, and people learned to appreciate this institution based in respect for the temporal order, the Anglican Church became a symbol of the English genius for compromise."

The Australian political tradition developed out of the British political tradition. Settlement politics is at the heart of one of the institutions central to this tradition: the Church of England. So, it is worth thinking a bit about the history of the Church of England as a settlement project in order to understand what settlement politics is and the place it has in the tradition that took root in Australia.

The Reformation in England

Everyone knows the story of Henry VIII's break with Rome because the pope refused to give him a divorce. This resulted in the English parliament passing the first Act of Supremacy in 1534. The act declared that the king – not the pope – was the earthly supreme head of the English church. Ironically, in 1521 Pope Leo X had conferred the title 'Defender of the Faith' on English monarchs starting with Henry VIII. The Act of Supremacy was enacted at the time of the Reformation, but Henry VIII was not part of the Reformation. He was content to preserve Catholic worship, doctrine, and governance – insofar as these were compatible with his headship of the church.

It was in the reign of Henry VIII's son, Edward VI, that the Reformation really came to England. Edward was nine when he came to the throne in 1547, and he was schooled in reformed theology by his chaplain, John Knox, whilst a regency council dominated by Protestants ruled in his name. Thomas Cramner, the Archbishop of Canterbury, came to embrace reform theology under the influence of Martin Bucer, a reformer forced to leave Strasbourg. Once the reformers were in the ascent, there were numerous changes including the abolition of the Catholic mass in 1549 and the introduction of Cramner's Book of Common Prayer to establish Protestant forms of worship in its place.

Edward VI's short reign was followed by that of his half-sister, Mary I. She was devoutly Roman Catholic and, upon her accession in 1553, she repealed all of Edward VI's religious legislation with the Statute of Repeal, and then repealed Henry VIII's Act of Supremacy in 1554 through the See of Rome Act, which restored the pope's authority in England. It was a time of great unrest, with three hundred Protestants burnt alive, including Cramner.

Catholic England proved to be a temporary state of affairs.

When Mary's half-sister, Elizabeth I, succeeded her, she enacted the second Act of Supremacy in 1558. This again abolished the authority of the pope and made the queen the supreme governor of the English church. The crown has retained its position as the ultimate authority within the church ever since. Yet Elizabeth was not the kind of Protestant ruler that Edward VI had been. To be sure, she insisted that, in order to hold any public office, one had to take the oath of supremacy, which meant one had to accept royal – rather than papal – authority was supreme within the church. Beyond that, she was prepared to tolerate religious disagreements about doctrine and theology – providing they did not threaten governance.

Doctrine, worship and governance

The separation from Rome was one of two major issues for the governance of the Church of England. There remained a second problem to be resolved. This went to the question of what kind of Protestant church was the English church to be. The Roman Catholic Church was divided into dioceses and each diocese was governed by a bishop. The bishop exercised legislative, executive, and judicial power in matters relating to the church within the diocese. Bishops also claimed apostolic succession; that is, they were part of an unbroken line that could be traced back to the disciples chosen by Jesus. This apostolic succession of the bishops gave legitimacy for their claim to power.

The Reformation involved challenges to doctrine, worship, and governance of the church. In matters of doctrine, one of the central disputes concerned salvation. It was agreed that belief in Jesus was a justification for salvation after death, but could *works* also contribute to salvation, or was it justification by faith alone? The Catholic Church maintained that works – or good deeds – could contribute to salvation, and this was the basis for *indulgences*, whereby wealthy people could give money to the church in return for remission of sins, a position that the reformers staunchly rejected. Questions of doctrine also spilt over into questions of worship. One of the most notable of these was the dispute over the status of the eucharist. It was agreed that Jesus had instituted the practice, but what did scripture mean when he referred to the bread as his body and the wine as his blood? According to the doctrine of transubstantiation, the Catholic Church maintained that the bread and wine actually became the body and blood of Christ once it was consecrated. This was a position that was fundamentally rejected by the reformers, who had different ways of explaining the sense in which Christ was present at the eucharist, but stopped short of believing that the bread and wine was transformed into the body and blood of Christ. This led to major changes in how Christians should worship, as did other disputes about the role of icons, ritual objects and clothing worn by priests. Another major dispute concerned the language of worship. Should prayers and bible readings be in Latin, a language that ordinary people did not understand, or should they be in the vernacular language? The reformers believed it was more important that the language of the people was used, rather than the exclusive language of the church. Some of those reformers were Catholics who believed that the church could extend its reach if the Word was understood in English.

Finally, there were questions that went to governance of the church. Who had the final say about how the church was run? The Catholic Church had claimed that the bishops had authority to run the church and that the pope had authority over all the other bishops. This claim was traced back through an unbroken line from the bishops of the day to the disciples chosen by Jesus, or what was called 'apostolic succession'. The reformers rejected this, claiming that it was the faithful together who had the authority to govern their church. They argued that there was no scriptural authority for bishops controlling their dioceses, and that a more Christian model of governance would see the faithful within local communities govern themselves. This might mean the presbyterian model of governance, which sees the church governed by a representative assembly of elders, or the congregationalist model, which has each congregation independently and autonomously run its own affairs.

These and other issues were seriously debated throughout Western Europe where the Reformation took hold. Their impact in England was unique because Henry VIII, although fundamentally a Catholic, needed to renounce the authority of the pope for political reasons. From Henry VIII to Elizabeth I, there was no question of abolishing episcopal governance of the church (according to which the church is divided into dioceses and the bishop is the ultimate governing authority in each diocese). Those who maintained that the church should not be ruled by bishops were no more welcome in the Church of England than Catholics, who denied royal supremacy. The Act of Supremacy and episcopal governance were the two non-negotiables in the Church of England. The king was the ultimate authority and, under him, his bishops exercised within their dioceses authority that could be traced back to the disciples of Jesus. Beyond these non-negotiable matters of governance, the Church of England became an institution that tolerated divergence in worship and doctrine.

Church of England as a settlement

Scruton explains that "in religion we feel most strongly about the things that cannot be explained, and pit mystery against mystery in passionate advocacy." The strength of the Church of England was to recognise this and to enable people to remain strongly exercised about the mysteries that matter to them and not concede these to anyone, whilst at the same time being able to avoid the conflict that usually arises when people feel the need to overpower their opponents. He writes, "Ours is a *settled* church, in which doctrinal differences have been marginalised, and custom, ceremony and unthreatening mysteries placed in the foreground." This settlement does not seek to resolve theological disputes comprehensively because it eschews statements of doctrine: "Anglican doctrine is not sharpened by Biblical exegesis and argumentative commentary, such as that provided by Calvin in his line-by-line exposition of the Gospels. It is softened through ceremony, and buried in the folds of a ritual cloak so that only its outlines appear."

For Scruton, the established church is fundamentally about ensuring civil peace. Through toleration, those who disagree about doctrine and ritual can go their own way so long as this does not permit a situation in which the external enemies of the kingdom can get an advantage. This worked to the benefit of (almost) everyone in the kingdom. Those outside the Church of England would have a longer wait for tolerance: 1689 for Nonconformists with the Toleration Act; 1813 for Unitarians with the Doctrine of the Trinity Act; 1829 for Catholics with the Roman Catholic Relief Act; and 1858 for Jews with the Jews Relief Act.

The Forty-two Articles written by Thomas Cranmer in 1553 set out the official doctrinal position of the Church of England in the reign of Edward VI as an unambiguously Protestant church. When, in 1563, Matthew Parker reworked these into the Thirty-nine Articles, he reflected the compromise that Elizabeth I sought. The more extreme Calvinist aspects were redacted and what was left was intended to be the basis for a compromise, that, in Scruton's words, "would extend the protection of the Church to all true Christians in the land, while defining the Church of England as an Episcopal and Apostolic church, against the competing claims of Rome on the one hand, and the Calvinist, Presbyterian and Anabaptist dissenters on the other."

The solution that emerged was a distinctive compromise that,

Scruton argues, owes much to the theologian and legal philosopher, Richard Hooker. Hooker's masterpiece is the unfinished *Of the Lawes of Ecclesiasticall Politie.* It is a defence of the Church of England against charges raised both by Roman Catholics and Puritans (Protestants who would have reformed the Church of England further, and whose successors, the Nonconformists, ended up leaving the church and establishing their own Protestant sects outside the Church of England). In doing so, Hooker also develops a distinctly Anglican theology. Whereas the Catholic Church gave scripture and tradition equal standing, and the Puritans recognised only scripture as a source of authority, Hooker argued that human reason is also relevant when scripture is silent or ambiguous. This gave Anglicanism its distinctive flavour that draws on scripture, tradition, and reason. Hooker's commitment to the role of reason in theology meant that he could conceive of a church in which reasonable and pious Christians could disagree. The church did not have to suppress one disputant, nor did it have to iron out points of disagreement by somehow blending them into a position that was acceptable to all. Rather, Scruton writes, it could accept that, within certain parameters, disagreement can occur without undermining the institution: "Thanks in part to Hooker's influence, the Church that emerged from Elizabeth's reign was an ecumenical one, not a synthesis of rival views, but a panoply spread over all those Christian obediences that could honestly accept the Act of Supremacy and the Episcopal government."

Scruton concludes that, for three centuries, the Anglican settlement was able to hold together a church containing people who disagreed with one another on any number of important matters. Admittedly, he has to deal with the fact that this Elizabethan settlement did not prevent a civil war between 1642 and 1651, which he and other recent scholars have described as a war of religion, but that does not detract from his broader point that the settlement reasserted itself at the time of the Glorious Revolution in 1688. To this day, there are the Evangelicals – or the low church – who prioritise the authority of scripture and the Anglo-Catholics – or the high church – who attach greater significance to ritual and tradition than the Evangelicals do. Admittedly less prominent now are the Latitudinarians – or the broad church – who emphasised the role of reason and promoted religious liberty within the church.

The combination of Henry VIII's break with Rome and the spread of Reformation thought throughout England created religious disagreement that, in turn, undermined the security of the realm both from threats within and without. There was a need to address this, and the solution was a settlement. In matters of governance, acquiescence was demanded, but in matters of ritual and belief, latitude was the order of the day. This was necessary given the religious diversity that had already established itself within England.

Strength and weakness of Anglican settlement

Scruton identifies two important consequences of this settlement. First, "the effect of the Elizabethan settlement was to create a church that had the broad endorsement of the nation, and a nation that had the broad endorsement of the Church." Secondly, "Moderation and compromise, seriously jeopardised in the seventeenth-century turmoil, became the default position of English institutions." These are things that he admires about the Church of England and its influence on English culture, but he also appreciates that they could not last forever. The seeds of its demise, Scruton believes, lay in its very purpose. He admires Hooker for grasping "both the community-forming and the community-destroying tendencies of religion, and the nature of a church, as an institutionalisation of both." As such, Hooker understood that a religious institution has, in Scruton's words, "two dominant duties: to *inspire* religious sentiment, and also to *contain* it." Scruton suggests that the Anglican

Church's great success in the second duty has extinguished the first.

The predicament is seen, according to Scruton, in the way the Archbishop of Canterbury's role has evolved from being the leader of a national Church of England to being the leader of a global Anglican Communion. He argues that the major disputes within the Anglican Communion in recent years – women priests and homosexuality – have not really involved English disputants, but rather have been prosecuted by American liberals and African conservatives "with the old English establishment looking on in mild astonishment at the fuss." Within England, the church no longer represents the "spiritual heart of the nation" and the Archbishop of Canterbury ceased to be clearly identified with the English settlement because, according to Scruton, "he had become head of a worldwide Anglican Communion, whose identity and beliefs were hostage to social and cultural changes over which the English Archbishop and Synod could exert no control."

Scruton argues that the Anglican Church no longer speaks to the questions at the centre of English culture. Its compromise is no longer one that holds together the rival tensions at the heart of the culture. Its settlement has become redundant in England and, in Scruton's words, its constitutional privileges have become "a kind of 'rotten borough' in Parliament." He sees in England's secular religion today a new ideology that is "less ferocious than the sectarian religions that fought each other to a standstill in the seventeenth century. But it is just as determined to triumph." The Anglican compromise has nothing to offer in this battle, however, and as such, he believes, "the English settlement has now disappeared."

Settlement and ambiguity

In its heyday, the Church of England was the archetype of settlement politics. In the sixteenth century, there was profound religious disagreement. There was a belief that religious disagreement could not be tolerated and, since the Reformation, the prevailing approach in Europe had been to wage war as a means of resolving religious disagreement. In England, religious disagreement was a genuine threat to peace. So, for the sake of establishing security within the country, it was necessary to find a solution. The idea that the Church of England could be established as a settlement in which Evangelicals and Anglo-Catholics could co-exist was a novel approach. It achieved the objective of maintaining security through creating a church that could allow people with different theologies to belong to it. Because the church did not claim to resolve theological disputes, it allowed people across theological divides to be faithful members of the church, even though their religious disagreements persisted. This arrangement served England well for three centuries until the religious circumstances changed due to the secularisation of England and new divisions emerged within the international Anglican communion outside of England.

That Evangelicals and the Anglo-Catholics could co-exist in the Church of England comes down to that church's capacity to embrace ambiguity in relation to doctrine and worship. Ambiguity, or the quality of being ambiguous, means being 'susceptible to more than one interpretation'. As such, it can also mean being 'unclear'. The word came into English in the early sixteenth century, when it meant 'indistinct' or 'obscure'. It comes from the Latin *ambi-* ('both ways') and *agere* ('to drive'). In Latin, *ambigere* means to 'waver' or 'go around', and from that comes *ambiguus*, meaning 'doubtful'.

Rarely, is it thought to be desirable for something to be 'unclear', 'indistinct', 'obscure', or 'doubtful' in politics. The quality of being open to more than one interpretation can be politically valuable, however, in some circumstances. Ambiguity, in the sense of being open to more than one meaning, can allow people to agree *that* something is important whilst disagreeing about *why* it is important. When a settlement draws on ambiguity, it enables people to explain their reasons for accepting the settlement in different ways.

Achieving this settlement was beneficial to England on two levels. First of all, it was convenient. The alternative would have been to suppress religious dissent which is a costly exercise – suppression of religious dissidents is never easy. But there is also a more profound reason. The settlement promoted a sense of tolerance that would eventually become the hallmark of British democracy. It is said that Samuel Taylor Coleridge was the first to refer to the Church of England as 'a broad church'. By this he meant that it could transcend the theological divide between the low church Evangelicals and the high church Anglo-Catholics. The church promoted religious tolerance and what might today be called 'inclusivity'. This is the great benefit of settlement politics. It enables the polity to resolve a problem in a way that leaves the polity less divided rather than more divided. To be sure, division still exists, but the solution enables divergent positions to co-exist peacefully.

Settlement politics in theory and practice

From the foregoing discussion, we can extract the following account of settlement politics:

1. There is some external pressure or situation that poses a fundamental challenge;

2. Although we all agree that the problem needs to be addressed, there is profound disagreement about the way forward;

3. In the circumstances, it would be better to identify a settlement than fight on until we can force our opponents to capitulate;

4. We can identify a settlement that involves some measure of ambiguity, which allows people to accept the settlement for different reasons;

5. This settlement is a response to the initial challenge and will only last as long as the challenge is perceived to last.

The three historical situations that we have discussed in this chapter and the last can now be understood as instances of settlement politics at play. The application to England is as follows:

1. Ongoing religious conflict presents a fundamental challenge to the security of the realm;

2. There are profound disagreements between Roman Catholics and Protestants, and amongst the Protestant sects, about how the conflict should be resolved;

3. The religious conflict cannot be quashed without excessive violence, which is neither realistic nor reasonable, so some measure of religious tolerance would be a better option;

4. The Church of England is a settlement that admits of ambiguity in matters of doctrine and worship but not governance, allowing for the tolerance of Evangelicals, Anglo-Catholics, and Latitudinarians (but not of Roman Catholics or Nonconformists);

5. When religious disagreement between Christians ceases to be a serious issue that needs to be managed in the national interest, the settlement becomes redundant.

In the Australian context, the challenges are quite different, but their resolution can be analysed in a similar way. First, Deakin's settlement and its persistence for eighty years:

1. The new Commonwealth needs a policy framework to consolidate itself as a new polity in the aftermath of the 1890s recession;
2. There are profound disagreements between Protectionists and Free Traders, and between all of these anti-socialists and the socialist-leaning Labor Party;
3. In the absence of an entrenched class system, there is no natural constituency for the parties, and the parliament is too evenly divided between these three parties, so there is a need for parties to find a compromise in the absence of any clear parliamentary majority;
4. New Protectionism and 'socialism without doctrine' is a settlement that admits of ambiguity in matters of social, economic, and industrial relations policy;
5. When the economic circumstances change in a way that aligns with the long-term free-market critique of protectionism, the settlement becomes redundant.

Finally, the politics through which this settlement was dismantled and replaced in the 1980s may be analysed as follows:

1. Changed circumstances in the international economy present a fundamental challenge to Australia's prosperity;
2. There are profound disagreements between the wets and the dries within the Liberal Party, and in the Labor government between those who are responsible for dealing with an imminent crisis and those who espouse fealty to the party's socialising mission;
3. The government does not have an electoral mandate for

this major economic reform, which will be difficult if the conservative opposition resists, and the opposition (whose shadow treasurer formed the view these reforms were necessary when in government) needs to hold its parties together, so some measure of agreement for these fundamental economic reforms would be desirable;

4. Piecemeal reform that is 'economic deregulation without doctrine' is a settlement that admits of ambiguity in terms of justification for reform and long-term objectives to be achieved through reform;

5. It is yet to be seen whether the free-market settlement has to be abandoned due to future changes in the international economy.

This analysis provides an account of what settlement politics is and how it has been applied to challenges relating to religion, challenges relating to the establishment of a new polity, and challenges relating to international economics. What this demonstrates is that settlement politics can be deployed to address a range of issues. The major challenges of today may be different. They include new challenges presented by Indigenous affairs and climate change. They are no less varied, but that does not mean that they are not susceptible to settlement politics. Whether settlement politics is relevant to how we address these challenges will depend on a range of considerations to be addressed in the second half of this book.

4

John Howard's Broad Church

Reflecting on Australian politics and his contribution to it, fifteen years after leaving public office, John Howard develops three themes in *A Sense of Balance* that are relevant to our understanding of settlement politics. First, there is his account of the Liberal Party of Australia, which he famously described as a *broad church*. In doing so, he was echoing the description of the Church of England, reminding us that the Liberal Party shares features of the Anglican settlement. Secondly, he offers his reflections on the nature of Australian society and the kind of public policy that it embraces. This he captures in the expression *a sense of balance*, which is another way of capturing the idea of compromise that is central to settlement politics. Finally, he discusses his own approach to bipartisanship when in opposition in the 1980s, and how this enabled the Australian Settlement to be dismantled through political agreement.

Liberal Party as a broad church

Since the dispute between the wets and the dries, the question of the Liberal Party's identity has been contentious. Howard had to deal with this as leader of the party in opposition. He has always maintained that the party is unique amongst centre-right parties as the custodian of two traditions: liberalism and conservatism. It was for this reason that he liked to think of it as a broad church. In the same way that Evangelicals and Anglo-Catholics were able to be faithful members of the original broad church, the Church of England, despite their theological differences, so too were liberals and conservatives able to be committed members of the Liberal Party despite their philosophical differences.

There are three senses in which Howard thinks of the party as a broad church. First, it is the custodian of two philosophical traditions; it can draw equally on each of these in formulating public policy. In this way, it cannot be strictly identified as either a liberal or a conservative party. He insists that the party is more effective politically when it is identified as the custodian of both traditions. As he writes in *A Sense of Balance*, "My long experience in the party has taught me that its unity, and ultimately its effectiveness, depend upon accommodating both strains of opinion within its broad philosophical base."

It is a liberal-conservative or a conservative-liberal party, and it can be seen as such even though there might be fundamental differences between liberalism and conservatism. Historically, this made sense because, when Menzies established the party, it was fundamentally an anti-socialist party, and, however nuanced the differences might have been, there were liberal objections to socialism just as there were conservative objections. Menzies himself was not doing anything innovative, but repeating the union of liberals and conservatives that had first taken place at the time of the Fusion in 1909.

That said, the second sense in which it was a broad church is that people who identified themselves as classical liberals or as conservatives could belong to the party and contribute to its success. The difference between the first and second conceptions of the broad church is that, in the first sense, we are talking about a party that is both liberal and conservative. In the second sense, we are talking about a party comprised of people, some of whom identify themselves exclusively as liberals and others of whom identify themselves primarily as conservatives. Despite all their differences, they can develop policy proposals that are acceptable to all of them.

The third sense in which the party is a broad church is more subtle. It is Howard's conviction that his own policymaking was a mixture of liberal ideas and conservative ideas. This he defended strenuously against charges that he lacked ideological purity. He saw no need for this. He liked to think of himself as a social conservative and an economic liberal. In this way, he seemed personally to embody both of the traditions of which the party was custodian.

His claim to being an economic liberal is somewhat more complicated than it first appears. As treasurer under Malcolm Fraser, Howard was an economic reformer or indeed an economic *radical*. He advocated fundamental change to the institutions underpinning Australia's protectionist economy. Fraser, by way of contrast, was an economic conservative. He sought to defend and uphold the institutions of the economic tradition. After the economic reforms of Hawke and Keating, the economy had been radically reformed from a government-controlled economy to a market-controlled economy. When Howard became prime minister, it could be argued that he was now an economic conservative because he was now committed to conserving and enhancing the established free-market institutions. Fraser and Howard were both economic conservatives as prime minister because they wanted to uphold and strengthen the existing institutions – it is just that the institutions had changed radically in the intervening period.

In another sense, Howard remained an economic liberal even if he was no longer an economic radical. This is because the radical reforms that had been introduced were in line with classical liberalism. As Fraser said in a speech to the Liberal Party's South Australian State Council in 1980, once liberal institutions have become embedded in the tradition, the liberal naturally becomes a conservative, because he seeks to conserve the established liberal institutions.

Australia's sense of balance

Moving from the party to the polity, Howard explains how he came to understand the character of the country, including its strengths and weaknesses. What he came to regard as a definitive hallmark of the Australian people is "that sense of balance in the formation of public policy that has long defined us as a people." Howard sees this sense of balance manifested in numerous ways, notably in the way the government and private sectors interact to deliver health and education services.

One of the clearest examples of Howard's sense of balance at play in public policy is the mixed system of public and private hospitals. Here we can see the positive role of ambiguity in policy. One might attempt to justify the mixed system empirically, by producing data that proves a mixed system is the most efficient. But such data does not go to the heart of the policy debate about what a mixed hospital system seeks to do and why this is desirable. It is here that the ambiguity comes to the fore. Labor politicians will tend to emphasise the mixed system as a means of ensuring that the most vulnerable are protected by having access to medical services. Liberal politicians will tend to emphasise the mixed system as a means of promoting individual choice. The mixed system of public and private hospitals is equally susceptible to either interpretation. This ambiguity is advantageous because it means that politicians across the political divide can support the policy. Of course, when Labor is in power it will likely reform the system to improve the safety-net features and, when the Liberals are in power, they will tend to reform it to promote the system's capacity for offering individual choice. Such disagreement about how it should work need not undermine agreement that, in principle, the mixed hospital system is desirable.

Howard describes it as a 'middle way', and this is a characterization that others have also suggested. He explains these compromises as "an even-handed treatment of fiercely contested points of view." This, he believes, is distinctly Australian, but it is an approach that is not only distinctive: it has also contributed to Australia's success, he argues. In trying to explain this, he identifies a sceptical frame of mind that he believes has insulated Australians against the more extremist social, political, and religious claims that their fellow citizens may make from time to time, whilst still respecting their right to conscience and faith. There is an "inbuilt wariness", he senses, that resists "the siren call of radical theories promising newly discovered solutions to age-old challenges." Albert Métin made a similar observation over a century earlier.

There is nothing particularly remarkable about these observations. They have been made before and are fairly uncontentious claims about Australia. A couple of points are worth making, however. First, this conception of the polity is as accurate a picture in the years that Howard was in parliament as it is for the earlier decades of the federation before he entered politics. A notable interruption, however, were the events of 1975. The Labor opposition boycotted the first sitting of the new parliament after elections that year. Mostly, the spirit of cross-party collegiality soon returned, however. More than that, it is, perhaps, a bit less unique than he suggests. These are features of the English tradition that took root in Australia. Secondly, there is a neat fit between the way Howard describes the Liberal Party and the way he describes the Australian polity. Thirdly, at his best, Howard exemplified a sense of balance in public policymaking. Towards the end of his premiership, however, this was less obviously the case when it came to industrial relations, with WorkChoices in 2005, and Indigenous affairs, with the Northern Territory National Emergency Response (the Intervention) in 2007. Such examples demonstrate that his sense of balance could desert him.

Howard's bipartisanship in opposition

As we touched on in the last chapter, Howard's conduct in opposition after the Liberals lost government in 1983 was critical to the settlement politics that enabled economic reform from 1983 onwards. He has acknowledged the "unspoken consensus" on many areas of economic policy before 1983, which saw the Liberal Party encourage employees to join trade unions during the 1975 election campaign, when Malcolm Fraser also announced that his government would "give Australian industry the protection it needs." By 1982, there was a public rift between the prime minster and Howard as treasurer, who was now clearly of the view that protectionism had to go and the industrial relations system needed to be reformed. As he writes, "Labor revelled in the political disharmony," but this was the beginning of the end of the cross-party consensus relating to government intervention in the economy. When, the following year, Labor gained government, it quickly found, like Howard as treasurer, that economic deregulation was necessary.

On floating the dollar, he writes, "I supported the decision wholeheartedly, and privately mourned the fact that it had been announced by a Labor Treasurer. Speaking on the ABC's PM radio program that night, I described it as both 'correct and courageous'." As shadow treasurer, Howard was prepared to promote bipartisanship in relation to economic reform: "In many ways the floating of the dollar and my immediate endorsement of it launched a period in Australian politics when the Coalition offered bipartisan support for a series of economic decisions made by the government. In most cases, this was because the ALP had embraced *our* policies."

In this instance '*our* policies' refers to 'Howard's policies', rather than 'the Fraser government's policies', because there was not yet agreement on the right about these policies. The deeper point, however, is that Howard did not oppose the policies: "I saw no point in doing anything other than supporting the government when it took decisions that I thought were economically sound. I resolved that the best method of responding to the new-look Labor approach was to argue that it should go *further* – in political terms, to attack the government from the right. It would hardly have made sense to do otherwise. Arguing *against* Keating's policies would have betrayed what I had argued over several years; it would also have caused intense disappointment to many supporters of mine, who saw me as the principal proponent of the cause of deregulation, greater economic freedom and smaller government."

In his own estimation, he did more than simply not resist reform – he enabled it: "Although Labor had shifted on floating the dollar and foreign banks, it remained adamantly opposed to abolishing interest rate controls – that is until I made it possible for the ALP to support this reform without taking any political risks." He offers the same analysis of higher education reform: "The end of so-called free university tuition, a holy grail of the Whitlam Government, was made possible politically by the Coalition in the 1980s when it called for the reintroduction of fees. . . There was some hostility from student bodies, but the support of the Coalition removed all the political sting."

The Liberal and National parties had gone on their own journeys in opposition; journeys that enabled them to support economic deregulation for their own reasons. Labor had often been hostile in opposition to reforms that it proposed in government. Howard may have been frustrated that he had not been able to implement the reforms when in government, but he conceded the importance of his opponents doing so when they were in government. He is also clear about the importance of the conservative opposition's support for the reforms: "They were good policies and those Labor governments deserved credit for pursuing them, notwithstanding ALP attacks on the Liberal Party when it first propounded them. They were all adopted with Coalition support. That support removed any political pain that might otherwise have occurred, particularly given that they overturned the conventional wisdom of decades."

In opposition, Howard had advocated for reform of the industrial relations system. This was consistent with his party's newfound ideological commitment to economic liberalism. The Labor government did not share this ideological commitment, however, and only implemented economic reforms when it was convenient, rather than out of ideological necessity. Labor did not share the ideological conviction, and Howard found that they attacked him when he called for workplace reform: "However logical such an approach might have been, it carried many political risks, and left me exposed to opportunistic attacks from both Hawke and Keating. *They* had the political luxury of picking and choosing how far to travel down their newly selected path of economic liberalism."

Howard as a settlement politician

In his approach to his own party, to the development of public policy, and to his dealings with his political opponents, Howard demonstrates an innate sense of settlement politics. This is apparent as much from independent analysis of what he did as it is from his own reflections on his time in office. To say that he exemplifies settlement politics is not to say that settlement politics is the sum total of his approach to politics. Indeed, it may be that he would not see this as a central feature of his approach to politics. There is plenty more to be said about his theory and practice of politics, and to agree or disagree with about these. Whatever one's final assessment of Howard, it is important to understand him as a settlement politician and to factor this into the assessment. And it should count to his credit.

Howard entered parliament in 1974 and experienced the last decade of the Australian Settlement, before, in opposition, participating in the settlement politics of the 1980s that saw the introduction of the free-market system, which he supported from the opposition benches in an act of settlement politics. He wrote *A Sense of Balance* a decade and a half after leaving parliament, so the book is as much a reflection on his time in office as it is a comment on the politics of today. What does he tell us about the prospects of settlement politics then and now?

Howard was able to identify conditions that presented fundamental challenges for public policy. As treasurer under Fraser, he became cognisant of the economic challenges. As opposition leader, he was required to acknowledge the need to address constitutional reform. He grasped both the immediate problem and the nature of the challenge in each case. With the economy, the challenge was to make substantive changes to institutions that were no longer fit for purpose, whilst at the same time reassuring people that the values of the Australian Settlement could be retained. In the case of the constitution, the challenge was to maintain as much of the constitutional machinery as possible – which the minimalist republicans believed worked well – whilst allowing for values associated with constitutional monarchy to be changed. He rightly saw that whilst the former could only be dealt with by making radical changes to the economy, the latter could be satisfied by allowing a public conversation about the constitution, and letting the people have their say. In one case, the challenge was actually to make the necessary change; in the other, it was to have a necessary conversation which may or may not lead to change.

He saw the need for economic reform and, although he couldn't implement it as treasurer, he supported it as shadow treasurer. He did not see the need for constitutional change, but he did see the need to be seen to be taking the issue seriously and committed to hold a constitutional convention. When the constitutional convention produced a model for amending the constitution, he agreed to put it to a referendum. He still did not see the need for change, and the electors ultimately agreed with him. What matters is that he saw that the circumstances required him to take seriously the call for a republic and to allow the Australian people to resolve the matter at the ballot box.

Since he left office, his successors have not shown his capacity for identifying problems. They have not demonstrated to the electors that they appreciate the seriousness of the problems and brought the electors on a journey with them. There was an almighty battle within the Liberal Party about whether climate change was an issue that needed to be addressed, and then, when it was resolved that it was, there was not the comprehensive resolution of the issue that there was when the wets capitulated to the dries.

Sexual harassment of women in the workplace, and other issues relating to the status of women, is another area in which the party has had difficulty. Whereas climate change involved the kind of profound disagreement that the free-market reforms also presented, there was not the same dispute within the party about whether there was a problem that should be addressed. In this case, it was more that the leadership struggled to communicate that it grasped the seriousness of the issue and that it was committed to addressing the policy challenges presented by it.

In Howard's day, there were profound disagreements about questions of high policy. It would be oversimplifying things to say that there have been no profound disagreements since he left politics, but it also seems that the nature of disagreement has changed. Often enough, objections seem to be contrived rather than profound. Howard was aware that he could have taken this approach when it came to economic reform. He could have taken the view that it was the role of the opposition to oppose and make life hard for the government. Instead, he acknowledged that this was the right policy and lamented that it did not go far enough. This line of attack assumes good faith on the part of one's opponent. Increasingly, as witnessed in critical disputes – such as those about climate policy – each side believes that the other is acting in bad faith.

Howard admits that the desire to settle rather than force opponents to capitulate is gone. He laments this and traces the end of bipartisanship to the era when Labor went into opposition. Labor refused to let government bills pass the Senate, even when there was an election mandate for the policy, as was the case with the GST. Understandably enough, Howard's contempt for their approach comes out in his writing. He notes that, as opposition leader, he did not insist on being obstructive. He writes that bipartisanship ended because Labor did not "repay the compliment." There is a lingering legacy of 1975 at play here. Nevertheless, Howard's general point holds.

Ultimately, Howard did not support the economic reforms as a courtesy. He did so because he had already come to see the need for reform. The end of bipartisanship no doubt has something to do with Labor's preparedness to be obstructionist in the Senate. But something else also happened. There was increasingly less willingness to find common ground. Howard did not have to agree with everything Hawke and Keating said, but there was enough common ground on the fundamental issues to allow him to want to let them get their reforms through. Over the last two decades, it is not parliamentary courtesy but the desire to settle that has changed most significantly.

Finally, does Howard's sense of balance provide the ambiguity necessary for settlement politics? It could well meet the challenge. Aristotle famously said that living well was a matter of acting according to the ethical mean. Unlike the arithmetical mean and the geometrical mean, which could be calculated mathematically, there was no formula for the ethical mean. The right action lay somewhere between the excess and the deficiency, but exactly where was hard to say. For some virtues, such as courage, the mean lay closer to the excess (rashness) than the deficiency (cowardice), but in the case of other virtues the mean might lie closer to the deficiency.

In ethics, this is easily criticised as a Goldilocks theory that does not tell us anything about what we should do, other than that we should not do too much or too little. When it comes to public policy, this vagueness can be a virtue. Achieving balance will involve some people on the left leaning a little to the right; and some on the right leaning a little to the left. This is not something that can be quantified. It is about allowing politicians the space to speak in their own political language and explain their reasons for policy reform in their own way. It means allowing one politician to be able to explain that a mixed public/private hospital system is best because it provides for those who cannot afford to look after themselves and allowing another to justify it on the basis that it promotes choice. They do not have to see eye-to-eye and agree with one another. They can continue to disagree about the precise point at which the scales are balanced. There will be enough overlapping domain, even if they choose to plant their flags in different spots.

So a sense of balance might be the right way to approach politics if one is aiming for settlement. The question remains as to whether politicians still aspire to a sense of balance, and, if so, whether the social conditions allow them to find it.

5

Losing Trust and Increasing Polarisation

Thus far, we have been looking at what politicians do when they engage in settlement politics. That is only half the story, however. If the politicians govern, then we also need to consider the attitude of those who are governed. At least in a democracy, those who govern are accountable to those who are governed. Settlement politics is only possible when people are open to compromise; people here being both those who govern and those who are governed. One recent report, as discussed immediately below, suggests that Australian society may be less conducive to settlement politics than it once was.

Settlement politics is only going to be possible in a society in which the people share an approach to living together that seeks to tolerate difference. If the people do not see the need for tolerance and making accommodations for one another, they will not vote for politicians who espouse such an approach. Rather, they will vote for politicians who present as warriors taking no prisoners and fighting to the death for their stance. Increasingly, Australia seems to be moving towards becoming the kind of society that cannot support settlement politics. The 2023 Edelman Trust Barometer is a good indicator of the direction in which things are going.

Decreasing trust

The Edelman Trust Barometer has been published annually since 2000. Edelman is regarded as the largest public relations firm in the world, based on revenue, having been established by David Edelman in 1952 and run by his son, Richard Edelman since 1996. Edelman's annual report measures the attitude of the general population in different countries to different kinds of organisations. In particular, it measures the extent to which people report that they trust governments, non-government organisations, businesses, and the media. The barometer is based on the responses of 32,000 people in 28 countries who participated in fieldwork conducted between 1 and 28 November 2022.

The trends in Australia reflect the global trends, however, it seems that the situation in Australia is deteriorating more swiftly. Australian respondents report that they are losing trust in institutions. Indeed, Australia reported the largest drop in trust – 5 points down on the previous year – and this was the largest reduction in trust of any country measured, such that now only 48% of Australians have trust in institutions. This moves Australia from the 'neutral' category (50-59%) to the 'distrust' category (1-49%). At the same time as they report losing trust, Australian respondents report that they believe Australia is becoming increasingly polarised.

Edelman is concerned with 'trust' as the means by which an institution gains the capacity to operate, lead, and succeed with stakeholders. Trust involves stakeholders' personal experience over the passage of time leading them to believe that the institution is agile, dependable, and relevant. In Australia, there has been a marked loss of trust in government. Government has entered the realm of 'distrust', with only 45% of respondents indicating that they trust government – a seven-point drop since 2020. Government is seen as a source of false or misleading information by 45% of Australians and as a reliable source of trustworthy information by 36%. In contrast, business is now seen as the only institution that is competent and ethical. This has created an expectation that business leaders will take a stand on social issues, and be visible in leading change.

Increasing polarisation

Edelman's headline finding in 2023 was that Australia is on a path to polarisation. Polarisation is the process through which opinions, beliefs, or perspectives within a society become more extreme or divided. It is more than mere division, however, as the separation between those holding opposing views is seen to become entrenched, giving rise to an 'us-and-them' mentality. Australia is currently straddling the boundary between being 'moderately polarised' and 'in danger of severe polarisation', with 45% of Australians believing that the nation is more divided today than in the past.

More than half of the respondents (61%) said the lack of civility and mutual respect is the worst they have ever seen. Astonishingly, only 24% of Australians are willing to help someone in need who strongly disagrees with their view on a societal issue; only 21% are willing to live in the same neighbourhood as people who strongly disagree with them; and only 19% are willing to work with them. The only good news is that there is still an opportunity to correct this course if action is taken to restore unity and trust before the country becomes severely polarised.

The general loss of trust in institutions, and in government in particular, is believed to have contributed to increased polarisation in Australian society. Edelman says that polarisation is observed to increase when distrust in key institutions is combined with a perception that there is a lack of shared identity, systematic unfairness, heightened societal fears, and economic pessimism. The situation is more complicated, however, because, although Edelman found that distrust breeds polarisation, polarisation causes further distrust as well as being a consequence of distrust. Amongst people who believe that their country is not very divided, 63% have trust in government. Amongst those who believe their country is polarised and that divisions are entrenched, only 27% have trust in the government. Thus, it is clear from the 2023 Edelman Trust Barometer that when we see our country as polarised, we don't trust the key institutions.

Trusting the trust barometer

The Edelman Trust Barometer provides a useful macro view of changes in Australian society, and it is worth thinking carefully about the implications of these changes. Before doing so, however, we should pause to consider a few ways that this big picture might distort our perception of what is going on. The tendency to simplify the key concepts, such as 'trust' and 'government', can be useful for making certain trends clearer, but, at the same time, it can obscure the nuance.

Edelman measures trust in 'government' and it contrasts this with trust in 'non-government organisations', 'business', and 'the media'. When carved up in this way, 'government' needs to do a lot of explanatory work. It can cover parliamentarians, public servants, judges, and perhaps the legal profession. This may obscure the fact that each of these could have different levels of trust. The fact that trust is rapidly deteriorating in some of the institutions of government might mask the fact that it could survive as far as other institutions of government are concerned.

The obvious target for loss of trust is politicians. Be this as it may, decline in trust of politicians might not equate to a decline in trust of the democratic state. Recent work undertaken as part of the Museum of Australian Democracy's Democracy 2025 initiative investigates federal politicians' perspectives on democratic structures. It reveals that whereas 61.2% of federal politicians are satisfied with Australia's democratic arrangements, only 40.56% of the general population are satisfied. The politicians are concerned about their constituents' lack of confidence, in particular their lack of confidence in politicians' capacity for community-linkage and integrity. Voters and politicians have differing views on how democratic institutions might be improved. The researchers were particularly struck by the fact that the politicians who responded to their survey did not identify the potential of digital politics or enhancing the relationship between politicians and the public service as resources for improving public confidence in democractic institutions.

The assumption behind the Edelman Trust Barometer is that trust is desirable and its opposite, lack of trust, is undesirable. Research undertaken as part of the Economic and Social Research Council's TrustGov project invites us, however, to think differently about trust. Rather than thinking about a binary distinction, its starting point is that there is a 'family' of trust concepts: trust, mistrust, and distrust. *Trust* is a positive evaluation based on empirical assessment of the government, combined with normative preferences, which instils attitudes such as loyalty, commitment, and confidence, and behavioural consequences such as compliance, sympathetic judgment, and participation. *Distrust* is triggered by an evaluation that involves a negative normative assessment, with or without an empirical judgement, and is associated with insecurity, cynicism, contempt, fear, anger, and alienation, and results in behaviours such as withdrawal, aggressive and populist challenge, or empowerment movements. *Mistrust* involves an evaluation activity that looks for actors, institutions, and systems to signal their trustworthiness. It involves cautious, watchful, and questioning attitudes, and sees people make an effort to be informed, alert, and on standby to act.

Although mistrust might seem like the opposite of trust, that does not mean it is undesirable. In fact, it plays an important role in a functional democracy. Whereas trust contributes to social cohesion and makes good governance possible, mistrust instils a sense of political scepticism in citizens, which encourages them to become politically engaged and to hold their representatives to account. In some situations, there is even a constructive role for distrust: if the government is failing to act in the interests of the people, then distrust can stimulate political activity that brings the government to account. The significance of this analysis is that whilst trust in government is desirable, it is not the only desirable attitude. Mistrust plays an important role in a functioning democracy, and, in extreme circumstances, even distrust can play a constructive role.

Having drilled down into what is being measured by 'government' and 'trust', a final thought concerns the challenges that we trust government to deal with. Even if we have trust in the government, do we think that the government has the capacity to address the challenges that we face? If people believe that the challenges are simply beyond the capacity of the government, then it does not matter how trustworthy the government is. Malaise might set in if people give up on politics entirely because they form the conclusion that the policy challenges are simply too big for the government to address. Political malaise, along with the role of mistrust and attitudes to different governmental institutions are examples of the range of considerations that we need to keep in mind beyond those canvassed by Edelman.

Threatening social cohesion

What cannot be denied, however, is that the decline in trust and increase in polarisation identified by the 2023 Edelman Trust

Barometer does present a new kind of challenge. In seventeenth-century England, the challenge was to maintain security in the midst of religious disagreement and political instability that resulted in civil war. In twentieth-century Australia, the challenge was to maintain prosperity, initially through artificial means, and subsequently by addressing changing international economic circumstances. The challenge that the 2023 Edelman Trust Barometer identifies is not a threat to security or prosperity – although it might indirectly lead to these – but to social cohesion.

This situation is not lost on Australian parliamentarians. In his maiden speech as federal Member for Menzies in 2022, Keith Wolahan drew the House's attention to the United States National Intelligence Council's Global Trends Report, which itself drew attention to the challenge posed by increasingly polarised societies. He took from this the paradox that as people have "grown more connected through technology, that very connectivity had divided us." He observed that this is creating "information silos" in which "beliefs are reinforced, and truth is subjective." He identifies two threats to democracy from this polarisation. First, "fragmentation has in part led to a gap between what people demand and what governments can deliver." Secondly, "trapped in our silos, we are tempted to exaggerate our own virtue and see the other as a cartoon villain."

More recently, in an address to the Royal United Services Institute Victoria in April 2023, titled "Our Race Against Time to Win the Battle of the Mind", the shadow minister for home affairs and cyber security, Senator James Paterson, drew attention to the serious threat that he sees for Australia's defence and national security as a result of the "major power competition in our region [that] has the potential to threaten our interests, including the potential for conflict." He is ever mindful "of the Chinese Communist Party's demonstrated willingness to deploy all levers of state power in pursuit of its strategic interests." In a wide-ranging discussion, he draws attention to the lessons that

Australia needs to learn from the war in Ukraine. He points to the way that Russia was able to run a digital disinformation campaign which nearly succeeded in undermining confidence in the Ukrainian authorities through fake stories about biological weapons allegedly being developed by Ukraine in secret with American support. Such misinformation was used "to sow discord and confusion and weaken Ukrainian resolve." He points out that this use of fake news as a source of disinformation is a particularly potent weapon in a country like Australia, where "citizens in liberal democracies have become disoriented and divided in a post-truth information economy, ultimately disengaging from the democratic process as authoritative sources of truth". For Paterson, the lesson is that Australia must take steps to prevent the opportunity for a foreign power – which he takes to include companies controlled by the Chinese Communist Party – "to sow division, undermine social cohesion, erode national unity and suppress inconvenient narratives."

Speaking to GB News at the Alliance for Responsible Government conference in London in November 2023, the federal Member for Canning and shadow minister for defence, Andrew Hastie, has similarly warned about the defence risk that the loss of social cohesion creates when a country is presented with a risk from a foreign power. Hastie argues that the social and moral consensus has collapsed over the last thirty years in countries like Australia as the society has broken into what he calls 'tribes'. He notes that authoritarian powers, such as Russia, China, and Iran pose serious threats, "but the challenge for us is if we're divided as countries, it's very hard to meet those authoritarian threats." When there is so little social cohesion, the lack of agreement about anything means "it's very hard to come up with grand strategy" for combatting foreign threats, he argues.

Combining the Paterson and Hastie analyses, there are two aspects to the problem. On the one hand, Hastie warns that the loss of social cohesion makes Australia less well equipped to respond to the external threats. On the other hand, Paterson warns that a foreign power can quite deliberately act to break down social cohesion in Australia as a means of weakening Australia.

Settlement politics and polarised politics

Settlement politics is predicated on tolerance. It assumes that although I might not have the same thoughts as you, or feel the same way about something as you, or share your desires for the future, I am prepared to accept and accommodate you despite these differences. It involves the quality of open-mindedness. It is to say that, within certain boundaries, differences of opinion, sentiment, or aspiration do not make someone *other*. Tolerance is about accepting that someone can belong to our community, or be *one of us*, even if that person does not share (some of) our beliefs, feelings, or desires. If we have the capacity for tolerance, then we can see why it would be desirable to accommodate difference. Tolerant people will be disposed to find settlements that accommodate different perspectives, rather than insisting that there is only one acceptable way to address a fundamental challenge.

A polarised society is one in which the capacity for tolerance has been lost. When disagreement is seen as a form of permanent division within a society, those who disagree with us are seen as *other*. Not only are their views regarded as unworthy, but the people who hold the views are deemed unworthy. In this way, the us-and-them mentality sets in, and, with it, a conviction that accommodating different perspectives is undesirable. Thus, a polarised society will not be conducive to a settlement that is predicated on tolerance.

We have seen that settlement politics enabled previous generations of Australian politicians to address the most pressing challenges the country faced, but is it capable of addressing the current challenge of eroding social cohesion? Can a broad church operate in such a world? Is a sense of balance possible? The settlement politics that we discussed in the previous chapters operated in a less polarised society. It is not clear that it is suited to a world in which people have no trust and believe that division is entrenched. If people are not prepared to live next to those who disagree with them, or work with them, or help them when in need, how can we suppose they will be impressed by politicians who strive to bridge divides?

We can hold fundamentally different views about the world and still reach settlement, providing we are able to characterize our opponents as *different* rather than *other*. Ambiguity can enable us to reach settlement with opponents whose views are different from our own. It cannot achieve settlement with opponents whom we regard as *other*. By the time a society has become polarised in the strongest sense, its members have moved beyond seeing someone who disagrees as *one of us* who holds different views to seeing someone who disagrees with us as *one of them*. Ambiguity is about making space for people to accept a settlement for different reasons because we see our political opponents as worthy of tolerance, rather than as enemies to be defeated. If we regard those who disagree with us as *other*, then no amount of ambiguity will enable us to find a settlement with them. Rather, we must defeat the enemy.

Edelman shows that there is a loop between decreasing trust and increasing polarisation, but it might be argued that there is a similar loop between settlement politics and a polarised society. Yes, it is harder to have settlement politics in a polarised society, but political leaders' abandonment of settlement politics will also promote polarisation. The question is whether preserving settlement politics is worthwhile. Is it capable of addressing the challenges of a polarised society, or is some other form of politics required?

In recent years, we have seen the emergence of at least two alternative forms of politics. Identity politics can be found on the left of the political spectrum in Australia and populist politics on the right. Both are marching towards the centre of the political spectrum. These approaches to politics are radically different from settlement politics. So perhaps we are at a crossroads – either we abandon settlement politics and prepare for a world of polarised politics based on identity or populism, or we address the threat of polarisation and restore settlement politics.

Identity politics

Identity politics might be understood as the successor to the American civil rights movement of the 1950s and 60s. That movement aimed at removing race-based discriminatory laws which prevented some people from enjoying civil rights extended to everybody else. Identity politics seeks to tackle discrimination in a different way. Its starting point is that there are groups in society that have suffered oppression based on some aspect of their shared identity – e.g., race, sex, or sexual orientation – as a result of political actions. In order to address this oppression, it is necessary to provide for the interest of these oppressed groups. When it comes to identifying the interests and how they may be addressed, only people with first-hand experience of the oppression are thought to be in a position to determine the interests. Thus, only those who share the identity are able to determine what political action is necessary in order to address the oppression.

Identity politics is problematic for a number of reasons. Liberalism and Marxism both maintain that there is some fundamental human nature that we all share, and that the aim of politics is to deliver for all of us – that we should all enjoy freedom or equality. These are universalist – they are about the idea that we all have similar human interests and that the state should provide for these universal interests. The original civil rights movement was consistent with this because its basic claim was that discriminatory laws were preventing some people from pursuing the same human interests that others had and were able to pursue. Identity politics rejects this starting point. It believes that a group has distinctive interests that are determined by their shared experience of oppression, and political action is necessary to address these distinctive interests, rather than to ensure that they are treated in the same way as everyone else.

It is not hard to see how such an approach to politics could flourish in an increasingly polarised society. People are encouraged to focus on the social groups with which they identify, the particular interests of those groups, and how these interests can be realised through political action. There is no imperative to consider the national interest or the common good. It is about our determining what 'people like us' need.

Populism

Populist politics takes its starting point from the division between those who exercise power and those over whom power is exercised. Those exercising power are called 'the elites' and those over whom power is exercised are 'the people'. Populists maintain that the problem with contemporary politics is that the elites are out of touch with the people; that they neither understand nor share the interests of the ordinary people. The challenge is then to remove power from the elites and replace them with people who understand or share the people's interests, and who will then exercise power in the interest of the ordinary people.

This is a style of politics rather than an approach to policymaking. In advocating for 'the people', populists identify threats that lie outside 'the people'. Depending on the substantive commitments of the populist politician, these threats might be internal, such as large corporations, or external, such as immigrants seeking to enter the country. In any case, 'the people' tends to be identified with a section of the population, namely the section that the populist politician seeks to win over at the next election, rather than with the population as a whole.

The elites are those who have gained control of the institutions through which power is exercised. These include the government, non-government organisations, the media, and big business. The 2023 Edelman Trust Barometer indicates that Australians have lost trust in the leaders of all these institutions. So it is not hard to see how an increasingly polarised society, in which people have lost trust in those controlling the institutions of power, would be ripe for populist politics.

It would be a mistake to suggest that identity politics and popularism are simply two sides of the same coin. When compared with settlement politics, however, certain similarities become apparent. These, perhaps, justify classifying both as forms of 'polarised politics'. They share features that are more conducive to a polity in which there is decreasing trust and increasing polarisation. Hastie has said that the 'social collapse' or lack of social cohesion that he has identified as a defence risk for Australia is a result of identity politics. This is partially correct, but it is not the whole story. Identity politics is one form of polarised politics, and all forms of polarised politics contribute to the breakdown of social cohesion. But polarised politics is also a consequence of the loss of trust and increased polarisation. So it is important to remember that people will be drawn more to identity politics if they experience a lack of social cohesion.

Settlement politics in a polarised society

Settlement politics is predicated upon broad acknowledgement of some genuine or profound problem that is a problem for the polity as a whole. Yet it is increasingly difficult to get consensus about problems when there is a loss of trust. With no acknowledged sources of authority, it is easier to disagree about what the problems are than to find agreement about how they should be solved. The populists will say that the elites are deceiving us when they trot out their experts to tell us what the problems are. Identity politics will insist that the problems that need to be prioritised are the problems of oppressed groups, not problems faced by the polity as a whole.

It is also central to settlement politics that sometimes the disagreements about how to address a problem are profound; that people's convictions can lead them to conclude that problems must be addressed in different ways. In a highly polarised polity, there is a tendency to contrive disagreement where profound disagreement does not exist. This is because polarised politics depends upon politicians reassuring their constituency that in an 'us-and-them' world, our politicians can be seen to stand with 'us' and not with 'them'. It does not matter that on some issues it might be possible to agree. It is more important to establish how we disagree. This leads politicians to be constantly looking for ways of disagreeing with their opponents, rather than scrutinising policy proposals to determine whether there are genuine objections.

When a problem can be solved, settlement politics prefers to find a settlement rather than fight the opponent to the point of complete capitulation. There is no interest in preventing the capitulation of opponents, however, in a polarised world. This is particularly so for identity politics which is committed to enabling the oppressed group to overpower the oppressive group. If there is no commitment to 'live and let live' when finding a solution, there can be no space for disagreement within consensus, which is the hallmark of settlement politics.

Through a measure of ambiguity, settlement politics is able to allow politicians to agree on a way forward despite at the same time articulating their contrasting views on public policy. Such ambiguity might frustrate those who insist on clarity, but this is the price that must be paid for the benefits of a settlement. If polarised politics replaces ambiguity with clarity, this might seem like a benefit. What actually happens, however, is not that policy positions are articulated with clarity, but often enough through banal sound bites.

Changes in the delivery of news are not the cause of a polarised society, but they have facilitated it. The 24-hour news cycle serviced by media outlets that provide a constant stream of reporting and commentary does little to nurture ambiguity in discussion of policy. There is little opportunity to develop considered policy responses to developing situations and even less time to articulate them. Often enough, there is only time to explain the point of differentiation.

Political parties are based on shared political values, and these values provide the basis for developing settlements and explaining reasons for embracing them. The decline in loyalty to traditional political parties creates a further challenge here. If people vote according to party loyalty, it is possible to use the party's shared political values to explain reasons for supporting a settlement. As people shift towards voting based more on individual issues, rather than according to party ideology, it is harder to foster the political ambiguity that allows politicians to make arguments based on shared values for supporting a settlement.

Finally, aside from not resolving policy problems through new settlements, both identity politics and populist politics are inclined to invite the questioning of received settlements. In the case of identity politics, this is because received settlements are the work of the oppressors; in the case of populists, it is because they are the work of the elites. In either case, the result is the same: received settlements need to be dismantled.

The warning of the 2023 Edelman Trust Barometer is that Australia is *moderately* polarised and is in danger of *severe* polarisation. It advises that there is still time to correct course and restore unity before becoming severely polarised. That poses a question for us about what kind of society we want to be. Are we content to let Australia become a polarised society? The fact that there is still an opportunity to address this means that we are also faced with another question: what kind of politics do we want for Australia? Do we want to allow Australian politics to become increasingly polarised, or do we reaffirm our commitment to settlement politics?

6

Indigenous Recognition as a Settlement Project

On 14 October 2023, a referendum was held to recognise Aboriginal and Torres Strait Islander peoples in the Australian Constitution. The referendum was not carried, having failed to obtain even 40% support from the electors across the country. The proposal that was put to the referendum started out as a settlement project. Understanding the failure of this settlement project is important for our understanding of the state of contemporary Australia. This chapter discusses how a settlement was developed in private discussions that served as the basis for a public conversation. The next chapter considers the public conversation and how that failed to sustain the discussion about recognising Indigenous people in the constitution as a settlement project.

Settlement politics of constitutional recognition

There was a fundamental challenge posed by Australia's 'unfinished business' in the journey towards Australia's reconciliation with its Indigenous peoples. There were calls for constitutional recognition from Indigenous people and, in 2007, the conservative prime minister committed himself to constitutional recognition as did the Labor opposition leader. So there was bipartisan agreement that, for the good of the country, it was necessary to find a way of recognising Indigenous people in the constitution.

There was also profound disagreement about how to approach this challenge. On the one hand, Indigenous advocates saw this as an opportunity to give expression to their aspiration for restorative justice. On the other hand, constitutional conservatives saw this as requiring change that would not disturb the constitution and the system of government that operated under it. Some people saw the value in a symbolic gesture to advance the cause of reconciliation; others wanted to be satisfied that constitutional reform would deliver better outcomes in Indigenous affairs.

For a referendum to succeed, a settlement was necessary. Because of the very high level of support necessary for a referendum to be carried in Australia, any proposal needs bipartisan political support and, to obtain this, it needs to be uncontentious. That would only be possible if there was a settlement between Indigenous advocates and constitutional conservatives.

A proposal was developed that sought to achieve such a settlement. Indigenous advocates led by Noel Pearson brainstormed with constitutional conservatives led by Greg Craven in the Vice-Chancellery at Australian Catholic University in North Sydney. The proposal that was developed was intended to have the necessary ambiguity to allow Indigenous advocates to explain it as a proposal for addressing Indigenous aspirations by recognising Indigenous people; and, at the same time, for constitutional conservatives to explain it as a proposal that addressed conservative concerns and upheld the constitution. It was an opportunity to address the legacy of race, which could be presented as an important unifying moment in the country's national life, or as an opportunity to ensure better policymaking in Indigenous affairs.

In this case the settlement did not come to an end. Rather, it was never implemented. It failed because the two key groups each rejected one of the conditions for settlement politics to work. On the one hand, many of the advocates for change came to reject the need for a settlement. They believed that the electors should vote YES at the referendum on the basis that Indigenous people called for it: political consensus was not necessary for this, they believed. On the other hand, the conservatives, who it was hoped would see that there was a way of addressing their concerns, instead came to reject the idea that there was a fundamental challenge that needed to be resolved in the national interest. They came to the conclusion that this was all just an elite agenda and that ordinary people did not want it and should vote NO.

The failure of Pearson and Craven's approach suggests that settlement politics may not be possible in contemporary Australia. What the referendum ultimately exposed was how polarised Australia has become. Was the settlement project a mistake doomed to fail? Or could it have been saved?

Howard and the genesis of constitutional recognition

The idea that Aboriginal and Torres Strait Islander peoples should be recognised in the Australian Constitution developed out of the earlier process of reconciliation. The thought was that, if Indigenous and nonindigenous people were to live amicably in Australia moving forward, one requirement was that Indigenous people should be recognised in the Australian Constitution. At the constitutional convention held in 1998, to debate how the constitution should be amended if Australia was to become a republic, monarchists and republicans agreed that if the constitution was to be amended, it should include recognition of Indigenous peoples. Only the previous year, such recognition had been recommended in the final report of the National Inquiry into the Separation of Aboriginal and Torres Strait Islander Children from Their Families.

In 2007, John Howard announced that if his government was returned at the federal election due later that year, he would hold a referendum to insert a preamble recognising Indigenous people in the constitution. In an address to the Sydney Institute, he said, "I believe we must find room in our national life to formally recognise the special status of Aboriginal and Torres Strait Islanders as the first peoples of our nation. We must recognise the distinctiveness of Indigenous identity and culture and the right of Indigenous people to preserve that heritage. The crisis of Indigenous social and cultural disintegration requires a stronger affirmation of Indigenous identity and culture as a source of dignity, self-esteem and pride."

In making this call, he explained that he had not had a sudden road-to-Damascus change of heart. Rather, his proposal, he maintained, was "little more than an affirmation of well-worn liberal conservative ideas. Their roots lie in a Burkean respect for custom and cultural tradition and the hidden chain of obligations that binds a community together." For Howard, this was also a matter of truth-telling. He said, "I recognise that the parlous position of Indigenous Australians does have its roots in history and that past injustices have a real legacy in the present." In pitching the idea of a referendum to recognise Indigenous peoples in the constitution, Howard explained that his aim was to address the national interest, rather than some sectional interest: "In the end, my appeal to the broader Australian community . . . is simper, and far less eloquent. It goes to love of country and a fair go. It's about understanding the destiny we share as Australians – that we are all in this together."

Rudd, Gillard and the expert panel

As things turned out, Howard lost the election and Labor formed a new government with Kevin Rudd as prime minister. Rudd had made a matching election commitment to hold a referendum, so there was now bipartisan support for the idea. His focus was, however, on the national apology to the Stolen Generations and this overshadowed any discussion of constitutional recognition. It was his successor, Julia Gillard, who appointed an expert panel to recommend how Indigenous peoples might be recognised in the constitution in 2010. The expert panel was chaired by Patrick Dodson and Mark Leibler and reported in 2012. It proposed four changes to the constitution which involved the repeal of sections 25 and 51(xxvi) and the insertion of three new sections: 51A (recognising Indigenous peoples), 116A (prohibiting racial discrimination), and 127A (recognising English as the national language and Aboriginal languages as part of the national heritage). The proposals were not, however, put to a referendum before Labor lost office.

Abbott and the heartfelt pact

In 2013, Tony Abbott became prime minister when the coalition won the federal election. Abbott had affirmed his commitment to constitutional recognition of Indigenous peoples before the election and again after it, when the expert panel's recommendations were already on the table. He was the prime minister who said he was prepared to 'sweat blood' for this. He liked the idea of a statement in the constitution that recognised Australia's Indigenous heritage, British institutions, and multicultural character. This, he believed, was an honest statement about Australia, and one with which all Australians could identify. Everyone's ancestry can be traced back to at least one of the Indigenous peoples who were living in Australia before 1788, the British, who came thereafter, or the subsequent waves of immigrants from other parts of the world who together gave the modern country its multicultural character. He also liked the idea that it would provide a one-sentence summary of what is distinctive about Australia in the modern world.

As prime minister, he addressed Australians for Constitutional Monarchy, whose executive director he had been before entering parliament. The assembled constitutional monarchists were representative of the larger group of constitutional conservatives who would be hesitant of any change to the constitution. He asked them to suspend judgement and be openminded about possibilities, saying, "We will get constitutional recognition and, when it comes, I suspect that it will take the form of a pact, a heartfelt pact between Indigenous people and conservative Australia."

In this way, it was acknowledged across the political divide that reconciliation was Australia's 'unfinished business', and that constitutional recognition of Indigenous peoples presented a fundamental challenge that needed to be addressed. And yet, whilst there was agreement that this posed a fundamental challenge, there was also profound disagreement about how to address the challenge. The disagreement went both to what kind of solution was required and to what were the risks that needed to be mitigated.

Expert panel's recommendations

To understand the disagreement, it is as well to begin with the recommendations of the expert panel. The panel recommended the repeal of sections 25 and 51(xxvi) of the constitution. Section 25 of the constitution recognises the possibility of the states enacting racist electoral laws and stipulates the consequences for states that enact such laws. This section is now redundant because the Racial Discrimination Act prevents such racist laws being made. Section 51 sets out the legislative powers of the Commonwealth Parliament which include, in subsection (xxvi), the power to make laws for the people of any race for whom the parliament deems it necessary to make special laws. Until 1967, this power contained the restriction "other than the aboriginal race in any state." This restriction was removed following the referendum in 1967. The parliament has used this power on a number of occasions, most notably in the case of the Native Title Act.

These are the two existing sections of the constitution that deal with 'race' and it was thought desirable to remove them on the basis that this is not a category according to which laws should be made in the twenty-first century. The expert panel also recommended the insertion of three new sections. The proposed section 51A would recognise that the land was "first occupied by Aboriginal and Torres Strait Islander peoples"; that those peoples have a "continuing relationship . . . with their traditional lands and waters"; that their "continuing cultures, languages and heritage" are deserving of respect; and that there is a "need to secure the advancement" of these peoples. It then granted the parliament power to make laws with respect to these peoples. This grant of power would replace the power lost by the repeal of section 51(xxvi). The proposed section 116A would prohibit any parliament in Australia from making a law that discriminates "on the grounds of race, colour or ethnic or national origin." The prohibition would be subject to a limitation. The new section would state that this prohibition did not preclude laws made "for the purpose of overcoming disadvantage, ameliorating the effects of past discrimination, or protecting the cultures, languages or heritage of any group." Finally, the proposed section 127A would recognise English as the national language of Australia and Indigenous languages as "the original Australian languages, a part of our national heritage."

In summary, the first of these new provisions gives expression to the special relationship between the Indigenous people and Australia, and gives the parliament power to make laws with respect to Indigenous people. The second provision prohibits laws that discriminate against any group of people on the basis of race. The third provision recognises the status of the English and Indigenous languages in Australia. What one makes of these reforms depends upon how one believes the fundamental challenge should be addressed.

Three approaches to addressing the challenge

There were three broad ways in which people conceived of a response to the need for constitutional recognition of Indigenous peoples.

The first conception of how to approach the challenge is that all that is required is a 'tidying-up' exercise. This is a matter of removing the sections that deal with race, but not doing anything else to the constitution. If this is what is necessary to address the challenge, then it is sufficient to repeal sections 25 and 51(xxvi), and maybe replace the latter with a new power to make laws with respect to Indigenous affairs.

The second conception of how to approach the challenge is that what is required is some new statement that gives expression to the special place of Indigenous people in modern Australia. This is compatible with the tidying-up exercise but would also include an additional statement, such as the opening preamble of the proposed section 51A, which explains the special relationship between the Indigenous peoples and Australia before the second half gives the parliament power to make laws with respect to these peoples.

Even within the second conception, there is a further disagreement. Is the new statement supposed to discuss Indigenous people alone, or should it talk about them in a broader context? On one understanding, what is required is a statement that gives expression to the identity of modern Australia. In doing so, it might mention the Indigenous peoples as the 'first among equals', and also mention other equally important aspects of modern Australia, such as its British institutions and multicultural character. On the other understanding, the statement should only deal with the status of Indigenous peoples and not any other aspect of modern Australia.

On the third conception of how to approach the challenge, the starting point is that the constitution is the rulebook for Australian government, which has allowed for the dispossession of and discrimination against Aboriginal and Torres Strait Islander peoples. On this understanding, what is required is a change to the rules to create a guarantee that gives Indigenous people reason to believe that the future will be different from the past. Such a guarantee is compatible with the tidying-up exercise and a statement that gives expression to the relationship between Indigenous people and modern Australia. One way of creating such a guarantee would be the racial non-discrimination clause in the expert panel's proposed section 116A.

In this way, we can see how a profound disagreement might arise between those who believe that the correct way to address the challenge is through a tidying-up exercise (e.g., the Institute of Public Affairs in its *Race Has No Place* pamphlet), those who think what is required is an expression of the status of Indigenous people in modern Australia (e.g., Howard in his Sydney Institute speech), and those who think that what is required is a guarantee that gives Indigenous people reason to believe that the future will be different from the past (e.g., Pearson in his Quarterly Essay).

Three concerns about risk

The other part of the profound disagreement involves concerns about risks that need to be mitigated. These were expressed by the constitutional conservatives who were concerned that nothing should be done that undermined the relationship between the institutions created by the constitution or the values that underpinned it. There were three sets of concerns raised, the most eloquent exponents of which were Julian Leeser, Greg Craven, and Greg Sheridan.

Julian Leeser, who subsequently became the federal Member for Berowra, was the most forceful critic of inserting a preamble into the constitution. His point was that the constitution is a practical and pragmatic charter of government that sets the rules and the limits on the exercise of public power. He argued that symbolic language and recitations of history did not belong in the constitution. His concern was that it might be used by the High Court to interpret the constitution and that this could have unforeseen consequences. He had plenty of support for the proposition that a preamble could be used to interpret other parts of the constitution. These included the views of the framers of the constitution (e.g. Quick and Garran), a scholarly article by Mark Leeming and Stephen Gageler (who would subsequently become Chief Justice of Australia), and Howard's constitution alteration bill for a new preamble in 1999, which also included a clause for a new section in the constitution explicitly stating that the new preamble could not be used to interpret the constitution (presumably because he had been advised that a preamble could be used in this way unless it was explicitly prohibited).

Greg Craven, the vice-chancellor of Australian Catholic University, was the strongest critic of the proposed racial non-discrimination clause. He dubbed it a 'one-clause bill of rights' and predicted that those opposed to a bill of rights would strenuously oppose it. The objection to a bill of rights is that it empowers (unelected and hence democratically unaccountable) judges to make broadly political decisions about whether a law is acceptable or not. In the Australian constitutional tradition, it is for (elected and hence democratically accountable) parliamentarians to make political decisions. Craven's point was that the proposed clause would require the courts to decide whether to allow a law that discriminated, because the discrimination served the interests of the group that was subject to the discrimination, rather than working against their interests. The law cannot provide an answer to such questions. They involve value judgments which, it is argued, should be made by parliamentarians who are democratically accountable. It is the democratic mandate that justifies the value judgements politicians make; judgements which may at times be highly contentious.

Greg Sheridan, the foreign editor at *The Australian,* was the strongest critic of any amendment that would result in unequal classes of citizenship. His starting point was that all Australians must be equal before the law, and that it is philosophically unacceptable for the constitution to single out any group of Australians for special treatment. Any amendment to the constitution that would give Indigenous people a right or privilege that other Australians do not have would be philosophically unacceptable even if no one else suffered a material disadvantage. A prohibition on discrimination does not violate Sheridan's demand for equality. Indeed, it affirms his philosophical position that the law must treat everyone equally. The problem only arises when the law allows one group of people to be treated differently, or when it gives one group a right that others do not have.

To this mix must be added the background noise which is harder to include in the mix of profound disagreement, but which created the context in which the profound disagreement played out. The first part of the background noise was heard amongst *some* Indigenous advocates and their supporters. This was basically the line that "We've been oppressed by you, so you should give us whatever we ask for if we say it's necessary to overcome the oppression you have caused us." Some nonindigenous fellow travellers supported this line too, believing that Australia had oppressed its Indigenous peoples, so, in order to address the challenge of constitutional recognition, the constitution needs to be amended in a way that

Indigenous people deem necessary for overcoming their oppression. The other background noise came from people who said, "We're all Australians, so we all need to be treated the same." This creates a fundamental challenge for any change to the constitution that singles out Indigenous people as a group distinct from the rest of the Australian people.

Referendum politics and need for a settlement

Given the bipartisan political acknowledgement of the need to address the fundamental challenge, despite the profound disagreement about how to address the challenge, was a settlement necessary?

There were two distinct reasons why it might have been thought that this profound disagreement necessitated a settlement rather than the defeat of those with alternative perspectives. The proposal for constitutional recognition gained bipartisan political support not only because there was a fundamental challenge that needed to be addressed. Time and again politicians across the political divide said that this would be a great unifying moment for Australia; that it would bring us together as a nation. Given that there was fundamental disagreement about how to address the challenge, it would be very difficult to create a unifying moment by fighting one's opponents to the death. It seems that if one wants a unifying moment to emerge from a situation of profound disagreement, the only way to unify the disagreeing parties is to negotiate a settlement with which each party can live.

There is a more pragmatic reason why a settlement was required in this situation. It has to do with the politics of referendums in Australia. According to section 128 of the constitution, the only way the constitution can be changed is if an alteration is passed by both houses of the parliament, and then referred to the electors at a referendum. An overall majority of the electors who vote must cast their vote in support of the proposed law. In addition, there must be a majority of electors in a majority of states voting in favour of it. In other words, the electors in four of the six states must vote in favour of the proposed law in order for the constitution to be changed. This arrangement effectively stacks the system in favour of the opponents of change. In order to defeat a proposed law, opponents need to get a majority of electors in three states to vote NO. In order to pass a proposed law, supporters need to get a majority of electors in four states to vote YES.

History suggests that if either of the major political parties opposes a proposed law, it is practically impossible to obtain the necessary majorities. Before 2023, there were forty-four attempts to change the constitution, of which eight attempts were successful. The eight successful referendums have tended to concern uncontroversial matters or enjoyed bipartisan support. Ultimately, it is this *realpolitik* of referendum that means a settlement is necessary. If the proposed law is put to the electors in an atmosphere of disagreement, it is practically impossible to obtain the necessary double majority. That is to say, whenever a referendum to change the Australian Constitution is contemplated, the proposal will have to be a settlement. History suggests that the electors will not vote for a proposal if they sense that there is disagreement about it.

In the case of constitutional recognition of Indigenous peoples, there was profound disagreement about how to address the problem. It would not be possible to defeat a proposed law's opponents at the ballot box. The only way to achieve the double majority would be to propose a settlement that addressed the different concerns and to ensure that this settlement was acceptable to both major political parties.

Speaking at the National Press Club in Canberra on 9 November 2022, Megan Davis, co-chair of the Uluru Dialogue, addressed the history of referendums which suggests bipartisan support is critical for success. She said that bipartisan support may not be as important as it used to be. Noting that the last successful referendum was forty years ago, she said, "Who knows what a radical impact social media is going to have on discourse?" Thus, she maintained that it was difficult to make an absolute judgement on the importance of bipartisan support at a future referendum. So there was an understanding amongst advocates that bipartisan support was desirable, but less conviction that it was necessary.

Chancellery Group's approach

After Greg Craven's damning response to the expert panel's racial non-discrimination clause, Pearson decided that he and his advisor, Shireen Morris, should pay a visit on Craven. Craven encouraged them also to meet with Leeser, who was working with Craven at Australian Catholic University at the time, and he in turn proposed that I join the discussion. As things progressed, Professor Anne Twomey at Sydney University started attending meetings of this group of six, which Pearson dubbed the Chancellery Group.

Central to the Chancellery Group's engagement was the activity of listening. Pearson's team needed to listen to the constitutional conservatives' objections to the expert panel's proposal, and to understand where they were coming from; that they weren't 'racists', but that they had genuine concerns. Pearson may not have shared the concerns, but he had to accept that they were legitimate concerns. Craven's team also needed to listen to the Indigenous aspirations that underpinned the expert panel's proposal. It was put to them that they must accept that Indigenous people have suffered dispossession and discrimination. Once that proposition was accepted, a question was put to them: "If you don't like the expert panel's proposal, then what do you think is a better proposal?" Once one accepts that there is a serious challenge that needs to be addressed, one has to set one's mind to finding a better proposal for addressing it if one cannot accept the proposal that is on the table.

What emerged from the Chancellery Group's private discussions was a package of reforms that was intended to serve as the basis for public discussions about a settlement. In order for the settlement to work, a measure of ambiguity was required so that, throughout the negotiation process, and, indeed, the referendum campaign, there would be enough latitude for people to talk about the package in different ways and in different political languages that showed how it addressed one set of political concerns or another set. There were four parts of the package. These are compared with the expert panel's proposals in the following table:

Challenge to be addressed	Expert Panel's Proposal	Chancellery Group's Proposal
Removal of race-based provisions	Repeal of sections 25 and 51(xxvi) of the constitution	Repeal of sections 25 and 51(xxvi) of the constitution
Power to make laws	New section of the constitution granting parliament power to make laws with respect to Indigenous peoples	Revise section 51(xxvi) to replace the current race power with an Indigenous peoples/affairs power
Symbolic recognition of special relationship between Indigenous peoples and modern Australia	A preamble recognising the status of Indigenous peoples at the beginning of the new section of the constitution granting power to make laws and a new section of the constitution recognising Australian languages	Extra-constitutional declaration of recognition
Guarantee giving Indigenous people reason to believe future will be different from past	New section of the constitution containing racial non-discrimination clause	New section of the constitution establishing an Indigenous advisory body

First, the tidying-up exercise: section 25 would be repealed. This was uncontroversial. It was accepted by everyone from the expert panel to the Institute of Public Affairs.

Secondly, the power to make laws on the basis of race in section 51(xxvi) would be revised. It was still uncertain what the new grant of power would be. The parliament needed to retain power to amend the Native Title Act and to make other laws relating to matters such as the protection of Indigenous heritage. This might be a power to make laws with respect to 'Aboriginal and Torres Strait Islander peoples' or 'Aboriginal and Torres Strait Islander affairs', or some other formula. What was clear was that there would be no restriction on the kind of laws that parliament could make under this head of power.

Thirdly, there would be symbolic recognition of the special place of Indigenous Australians in modern Australia. This would not be contained within the constitution, but rather in an extra-constitutional declaration. It was still uncertain what the content of the declaration would be, but this was now a matter of political rather than legal considerations. By moving it out of the constitution, Leeser's concerns were addressed. He and I had published a pamphlet, *The Australian Declaration of Recognition*, setting out our proposal for a declaration that could be adopted through a popular vote. The gist of our paper was derived from United States Supreme Court Justice Antonin Scalia's observation that the Constitution of the United States of America is a practical and pragmatic charter of government, whereas the American Declaration of Independence is a statement of aspirations. In Australia, the constitution is also a practical and pragmatic charter of government. What is missing in Australia is a statement of aspirations akin to the Declaration of Independence. Our proposal was that Australians should adopt a statement of the country's history and aspirations through a plebiscite without changing the constitution. We did not propose what the declaration should say, but rather a public process for arriving at the text of a declaration. This proposal was fed into the policy mix though a submission we made to the parliament's joint select committee to consider the expert panel's report, chaired by Liberal MP Ken Wyatt and Labor Senator Nova Peris in 2015.

Fourthly, there was the guarantee. Having accepted that the racial non-discrimination clause would enflame the constitutional conservatives because it disturbed the balance between the Commonwealth Parliament and the High Court, a different kind of guarantee was proposed. Rather than allowing a court to strike down any parliament's legislation if the court concluded that it discriminated against a group without advancing that group's interests, the guarantee would now be that the Commonwealth Parliament would have to consider the advice of Indigenous people before making laws about Indigenous affairs. Noel Pearson introduced this idea in his 2014 Quarterly Essay, *A Rightful Place*, when he proposed that the constitution should be amended to make provision for an Indigenous body to advise the parliament on laws relating to Indigenous people. Exactly how this body would work, and how the constitution would provide for it, was not spelled out. Assuming there was interest in creating such a guarantee, these were matters for further discussion. The basic idea was that the constitutional relationship between the Commonwealth Parliament, the Executive Government of the Commonwealth, and the High Court would remain the same, whilst the constitution could make provision for a new Indigenous institution that would be able to provide advice to the parliament and the executive. This would create an obligation to hear Indigenous voices in Indigenous affairs and, in doing so, would address the grievance that past governments and parliaments had made laws and policies about Indigenous people without consulting them. It would give Indigenous people reason to believe that the future will be different from the past.

Political ambiguity and constitutional certainty

What this package represented was the starting point for a public conversation. It spoke to the range of concerns that had been expressed to date. It provided a basis for discussion that possessed the necessary political ambiguity for people to talk about it in different ways. It could be understood as a way of achieving better policy outcomes in Indigenous affairs or a way of recognising the rightful place of Indigenous people in the country's national life. It could variously be pitched as an opportunity to rid the constitution of the category of 'race', an opportunity to acknowledge the country's history, or an opportunity to address the grievances of a group who had endured dispossession and discrimination. This is the virtue of political ambiguity: it allows a proposal to speak to a range of political values. Once there was some level of acceptance that a package like this was required, the conversation could then move to how drafting provides constitutional certainty whilst maintaining the necessary political ambiguity.

The group had also been working on the drafting of constitutional amendments. The repeal of section 25 was a simple matter. Recasting the race power as an Indigenous affairs power was not too tricky. The question of symbolic recognition was now taken out of the constitution, so that was not an issue. The challenge was the amendment that would create the guarantee through an Indigenous advisory body. The group workshopped numerous options and arrived at drafting that addressed the concerns of the Indigenous advocates and the constitutional conservatives. The suggested drafting was published in 2015 by Anne Twomey on The Conversation website.

Twomey's drafting was for a new section 60A that consisted of four subsections. First, it established a new body with "the function of providing advice to the Parliament and the Executive Government on matters relating to Aboriginal and Torres Strait Islander peoples." Secondly, it gave the parliament power to make laws with respect to all aspects of the new body. Thirdly, it required that the body's advice be tabled in both houses of parliament. Finally, it required the House of Representatives and the Senate to give consideration to the tabled advice "in debating proposed laws with respect to Aboriginal and Torres Strait Islander peoples."

The drafting was supposed to demonstrate that the constitution could guarantee that Indigenous voices would be heard by law and policymakers when it came to Indigenous affairs. The drafting was designed to place the new body under the control of the parliament, and to ensure that the courts would defer to the parliament. The courts would not be able to strike down legislation and the new body would not be able to prevent the parliament from passing laws. The parliament would establish how the new body was to provide advice to the parliament and the executive on *matters relating to* Indigenous peoples, but the parliament would be required to consider advice when debating *proposed laws with respect to* Indigenous people. The obligation, thus, applied to a narrower category than the overall function of the body.

It was argued that an amendment like this would not violate Sheridan's equal treatment requirement. If the constitution gives the parliament power to make laws with respect to a specific group of people, it is reasonable that that group's opinions should be heard before the law is made. Where things get trickier concerns the 'scope' question. What counts as a *matter relating to Indigenous peoples*? There are plenty of matters that *affect* Indigenous people just as those matters affect all other Australians. The unequal treatment objection would arise if the provision enabled Indigenous people's advice to be provided in matters that also affected other Australians who were not guaranteed the same opportunity to provide advice. The Chancellery Group were satisfied that it was possible to settle on drafting that avoided the unequal treatment objection once the conversation got underway.

The Chancellery Group's work showed that it was possible to achieve both political ambiguity and constitutional certainty. This meant that it ought to be possible to reach a settlement. In order to arrive at a settlement, however, it was necessary to start a public conversation about finding common ground. If the public conversation proceeded correctly, it would use the Chancellery Group's work as the starting point for the conversation about finding common ground. Exactly where the common ground lay could only be determined after the public conversation got under way.

Referendum council's public conversation

In 2014, the Aboriginal and Torres Strait Islander Act of Recognition Review Panel provided a report to Tony Abbott recommending the appointment of a referendum council to "advise on the final proposition and gain agreement to it from Indigenous peoples, constitutional experts, parliaments and the wider public." Abbott accepted this recommendation and his plan was for the referendum council to report jointly to the prime minister and opposition leader, thereby maintaining a genuinely bipartisan approach. Such an approach had the capacity to arrive at a settlement that enjoyed the widest support.

As it happened, Abbott's premiership ended in 2015, when he was replaced by Malcolm Turnbull. It was then Turnbull who, together with the opposition leader, Bill Shorten, appointed the referendum council. It was chaired by the two men who had chaired the expert panel, Mark Leibler and Patrick Dodson (who was later replaced by Patricia Anderson, when he became a senator).

As the referendum council began its work, there were two challenges that needed to be addressed in tandem. On the one hand, there needed to be a process for establishing an Indigenous consensus. If Indigenous people were to be recognised, it had to be in a way that had their support. So the referendum council's priority quickly became establishing an Indigenous mandate for one approach to constitutional recognition. The second challenge was to stimulate greater discussion that would expose a range of perspectives that needed to feed into a public discussion if a settlement was to be achieved.

Starting a conversation on the centre-right

Ultimately, a public process was needed for arriving at a settlement, but there was also a role for civil society in getting to the point at which a public process such as a constitutional convention might be held. Australians who cared about this issue needed to start having conversations. Julian Leeser and I established a civil society organisation, under the name Uphold & Recognise, to encourage such conversations. It was to be a conservative voice committed both to upholding the constitution and recognising Indigenous people in it. The conviction underpinning this initiative was that the two commitments were not mutually exclusive, but required openness to finding solutions that satisfied both requirements.

Uphold & Recognise needed to articulate the conservative case for why constitutional recognition of Indigenous people was a fundamental challenge that needed to be addressed in the national interest. It also needed to articulate the legitimate concerns that conservatives had about changing the constitution, and the profound disagreement about how to address the fundamental challenge. If it could do this, it would be able to help steer the discussion towards a settlement.

The charter of Uphold & Recognise acknowledged that those who came together to back it had different views about what needed to be done:

- Some of us hold such recognition to be a deep moral imperative;
- Some of us regard it as necessary for improving Indigenous health and education, which are the real priorities;
- Some of us believe the issue needs to be resolved and taken off the agenda once and for all;
- Some of us wish to identify the least worst option for addressing this issue.

Charter signatories included the great and the good of Australian public life: Dame Marie Bashir, Sir Angus Houston, Major General Peter Arnison, Peter Baume, John Fahey, Nick Greiner, Sir David Smith, Brendan Nelson, and Andrew Robb. These people did not necessarily share the same concerns, but they supported the idea that it was possible to find a way of recognising Indigenous people whilst at the same time upholding the constitution. Their concerns needed to be part of the mix if the country was to arrive at a settlement.

In 2016, Melbourne University Press published *The Forgotten People: Liberal and conservative approaches to recognising indigenous peoples*. It was launched by former Victorian premier Jeff Kennett, and included chapters by a range of authors who were sympathetic to the approach of Uphold & Recognise. They were broadly supportive of addressing the fundamental challenge of constitutional recognition, although they also reflected aspects of the profound disagreement about how it should be achieved. Contributors included former governor-general Major General Michael Jeffery, Australian Christian Lobby managing director

Lyle Shelton, former Australian Human Rights Commissioner Tim Wilson MP, former Australians for Constitutional Monarchy convenor Lloyd Waddy KC, Cardinal George Pell, and psephologist Malcolm Mackerras. Their contributions articulated different perspectives and different reasons for wanting to find common ground for recognising Indigenous peoples in the constitution.

Aside from the questions about upholding the constitution, there were also issues about what kind of entity was to be created in order to hear Indigenous voices. Concern was starting to develop that the proposed national advisory body would be top-heavy; that it would not be sufficiently anchored in the local communities that needed to be served. Warren Mundine was, at this time, a supporter of constitutional recognition – if the right model could be identified – although he subsequently became a campaigner for the NO case. He published a paper in 2017 titled *Practical Recognition from the Mobs' Perspective.* It was the first attempt for a 'ground-up' rather than a 'top-down' approach. He argued that what was needed was a guarantee that local bodies would be established to enable the people on the ground to be heard. He argued that establishing a series of local bodies, rather than a national body, would "realise the ambition of Indigenous Australians for self-determination and the mainstream ambition that Indigenous Australians take responsibility for improving their welfare."

As the public discussion ramped up, the challenge was to ensure that the profound disagreement amongst this range of voices was being heard. Only in this way would the public conversation arrive at a settlement that possessed the constitutional certainty and political ambiguity for addressing the broadest range of approaches. Such a settlement, it was hoped, would enable bipartisan support for the final proposal to be put to a referendum.

7

Testing Settlement Politics at the 2023 Referendum

"Let the record show in the referendum, we most certainly crashed," Mick Gooda, a former member of the Australian Human Rights Commission and the Royal Commission into the Protection and Detention of Children in the Northern Territory, told the Aboriginal National Press Club on 23 February 2024, four months after the referendum. He said the prime minister and the government had adopted a "crash or crash through" approach and ignored the normal rules of politics in putting the proposal to a referendum in the way that they did. He described bipartisan support as one of the "key ingredients" for success, explaining, "Some people describe politics as the skillful use of blunt objects, while others talk about politics being the art of compromise."

Without knowing it, Gooda was making the case for settlement politics and lamenting the failure to embrace it in the months and years leading up to the referendum. The last chapter discussed the way in which private discussions about constitutional recognition developed into a settlement project in 2014-16. This chapter considers the public discussions from 2017 to 2023 and the failure to maintain the discussion as a settlement project.

Referendum council's recommendations

The referendum council's terms of reference were to "lead the process for national consultations and community engagement about constitutional recognition, including a concurrent series of Indigenous-designed and led consultations." This consultation and engagement needed to do at least two things. First, it needed to establish that there was agreement at the national level that constitutional recognition of Indigenous people was a fundamental challenge that needed to be addressed. Secondly, it needed to identify the profound disagreement at the national level about how it should be addressed. Having done those two things, the council had to make a choice. It either needed to engage in a process of identifying a settlement with the ambiguity necessary for people who profoundly disagree about how to address the problem to accept the settlement for different reasons, or it had to recommend that the next stage was for the prime minister and opposition leader jointly to initiate such a process.

True to its terms of reference, the council's Indigenous members were given carriage of a comprehensive series of Indigenous-designed and led regional dialogues around Australia. These culminated in the 2017 national constitutional convention of Aboriginal and Torres Strait Islander peoples, which was constituted by delegates from each of the regional dialogues. It issued the Uluru Statement from the Heart, which was presented as representing an Indigenous consensus position. The Uluru Statement called for "the establishment of a First Nations Voice enshrined in the Constitution" and "a Makarrata Commission to supervise a process of agreement-making between governments and First Nations and truth-telling about our history." 'Makarrata' is a Yolngu word that means 'coming together after a struggle.' It first entered into political discourse in 1979, when the National Aboriginal Conference recommended a treaty of commitment be negotiated between the federal government and the Indigenous peoples and called its proposal a *makarrata*.

The referendum council's recommendations followed the consensus position at the constitutional convention. It recommended "that a referendum be held to provide in the Australian Constitution for a representative body that gives Aboriginal and Torres Strait Islander First Nations a Voice to the Commonwealth Parliament." It elaborated upon this recommendation by explaining that the functions of the new body should be set out in legislation, and that these should include monitoring the use of the race power (section 51(xxvi)) and the territories power (section 122). It also noted that the scope of the matters about which advice was to be provided remained contentious. Its only other recommendation was the adoption of a declaration of recognition outside the constitution to deal with the symbolic issues.

These recommendations were based on the deliberations of the constitutional convention held under the aegis of the referendum council. The difficulty was that, while this constitutional convention had succeeded in articulating an Indigenous consensus position, there had been no national constitutional convention that included nonindigenous people. There had not yet been any deliberative public process that involved Indigenous peoples, constitutional experts, parliaments, and the wider public as anticipated in the recognition act review committee's report. The recommendations of the referendum council could not, therefore, be said to be the result of a process for national consultation. There was no national convention at which the range of different perspectives could be ventilated in the way that Indigenous perspectives were ventilated through the regional dialogue process. What was needed was a national constitutional convention at which deliberation about the Indigenous consensus position could arrive at a settlement for addressing it.

The emphasis throughout the referendum council process had been on achieving an Indigenous consensus position. This was a necessary condition for a referendum, but it was not a sufficient condition for it. It was critical to establish that there was a consensus that the Indigenous wanted a guarantee in the constitution, and that their preference was for a guarantee in the form of an advisory body rather than a racial non-discrimination clause. It was also important to establish that there was Indigenous consensus that this had to come first, and then after a referendum, discussions about arrangements for agreement-making and truth-telling could follow.

What remained to be achieved? Beyond Indigenous communities, there was no broad agreement about the need for any kind of constitutional guarantee. Although there was broad agreement about the need to recognise Indigenous peoples in the constitution, it was far from clear that the way to do this was to create a guarantee in the constitution that gave Indigenous people reason to believe that the future would be different from the past. This was a result of the failure to engage with the range of different perspectives that nonindigenous people brought to this issue, or to recommend a deliberative process to do that as the next stage. Instead, attention had focused on the need to respond to the Uluru Statement, rather than on the need to arrive at a settlement for doing so.

Maintaining a bipartisan process

Malcolm Turnbull formally announced the government's response to the council's final report on 26 October 2017. The government would not be acting on the recommendations because it did not believe the proposal was "either desirable or capable of winning acceptance in a referendum." He noted that no detail was provided in the report as to how the proposed body would be constituted or "how the diversity of Indigenous circumstance and experience could be fairly or democratically represented." Aside from that, the government did not believe the proposal "has any realistic prospect of being supported by a majority of Australians in a majority of States."

The prime minister's response was a huge blow to Indigenous advocates. It was the first time in the decade since Howard put constitutional recognition on the agenda that the government had unequivocally rejected a formal recommendation. There was no ambiguity in the response. There was no sense in which the government was indicating that it wanted to try and find common ground in relation to this recommendation. The response also risked jeopardising the bipartisan spirit in which the referendum council had been appointed. A decade of bipartisanship was in peril as the government became estranged from the Indigenous advocates.

To continue the bipartisan process, the prime minister and opposition leader agreed to establish a second joint select committee of the parliament to consider the existing body of work in the expert panel's report and the previous joint select committee's, as well as that of the council. The new committee was chaired by Liberal MP Julian Leeser and Labor Senator Patrick Dodson. Their committee found that there was very little consensus about what a First Nations Voice was or how it would operate in practice. The committee recommended a process through which the government and Indigenous people would co-design a First Nations Voice. This would give greater clarity to what the new body would be. The committee also noted that there was no consensus about how to draft an amendment to enshrine the new body in the constitution, with no less than eighteen suggestions having been proposed in submissions. It recommended that "following a process of co-design, the Australian Government consider, in a deliberate and timely manner, legislative, executive and constitutional options to establish The Voice."

In 2018, Scott Morrison replaced Turnbull as prime minister. He adopted the joint select committee's recommendations as an election promise in 2019. If his government was returned at the election later that year, he would commence the co-design process and would defer a decision about the question of constitutional recognition until after the co-design process was completed.

After Morrison's government was returned at the election, the new minister for Indigenous Australians, Ken Wyatt, established a co-design process led by Marcia Langton and Tom Calma. They were to oversee a process for advising on options for models that would ensure that Indigenous Australians are heard at all levels of government. Following the advice of the Dodson-Leeser committee, constitutional issues were to be treated separately. How the constitution might be amended was a matter to be considered after the Voice had been designed.

There was criticism from Indigenous advocates that discussion about constitutional recognition should not have been put on hold whilst the co-design process occurred, but the reality was that this was a complicated enough process without adding the extra dimension of the constitution into the mix. Committees were established to examine what mechanisms were required for Indigenous communities to engage constructively with governments at the local, regional, and national levels. Some stakeholders valued a model that was more top-down, whereas others valued something that was ground-up. The critical issue was whether a national entity was to be established, which then made provision for Indigenous people to be heard at local and regional levels, or whether the starting point was local entities, which then came together at the national level. What was clear was that any successful model required the capacity to work effectively at all three levels.

Conversations about finding common ground

Discussion about constitutional issues did not cease during this time. In particular, an important paper was given by Murray Gleeson, who had been appointed as Chief Justice of Australia by John Howard. In his 2019 paper, *Recognition in keeping with the Constitution*, this constitutional conservative made the argument for why reform was in order and why it could be achieved without disturbing the way that the constitution distributed power. He said, "It is unlikely that Parliament will propose a change to the Constitution in aid of Indigenous recognition if the effect of the change will be to curtail its own legislative power. That appears to have been well understood by the supporters of the Voice." Within these constraints, he saw the value of constitutional reform: "A Voice to Parliament has the merit that it is substantive, and not merely ornamental. It is not aimed at assuaging the sensibilities of some non-Indigenous people. It would give Indigenous people a constitutionally entrenched, but legislatively controlled, capacity to have an input into the making of laws about Indigenous people or Indigenous affairs." Gleeson seemed to understand that this was a settlement project and a proposal that was the kind of gradual change that Edmund Burke had articulated as the conservative vision of reform. In Gleeson's words, "A proposal that the Constitution should provide for Parliament to design, establish, and determine from time to time the make-up and operations of a body to represent Indigenous people, with a specific function of advising about the exercise of that power, hardly seems revolutionary."

It was hoped that a speech like this would help constitutional conservatives to open their minds to possibilities that could be acceptable to them. The drafting that Anne Twomey had published in 2015 had not garnered the kind of broad support that it was hoped it might achieve. Opinion was divided, but certain insiders were confident that the Twomey 2015 amendment had been comprehensively rejected by the Turnbull government, and that this remained the position of the Morrison government. In 2020, Twomey published two more suggestions for ways that the constitution might be amended to create an obligation for the parliament to make provision for Indigenous voices to be heard. This was part of an attempt to show that a compromise might still be possible; that there were different ways of drafting an amendment, and that people who were unable to support one version might nevertheless be able to support another.

The first of Twomey's 2020 suggestions was a revision of the race power. She suggested that section 51(xxvi) could be amended to give the parliament power to make laws with respect to "Aboriginal and Torres Strait Islander peoples; and in relation thereto, the interaction between Aboriginal and Torres Strait Islander peoples and the Parliament and Government of the Commonwealth." Her second suggestion was that a new section could be inserted in the constitution along the following lines: "The Commonwealth shall make provision for Aboriginal and Torres Strait Islander peoples to be heard by the Commonwealth regarding proposed laws and other matters with respect to Aboriginal and Torres Strait Islander affairs, and the Parliament may make laws to give effect to this provision."

Kerry Pinkstone, who had carriage of these issues in the prime minister's office during the Turnbull premiership published a paper aimed at helping to restart the stalled constitutional discussion in 2020. In *Anchoring our Commitment in the Constitution*, she took as her starting point the Liberals' longstanding commitment to constitutional recognition, the Uluru Statement's call for a First Nations Voice guaranteed by the constitution, and the policy position of the Turnbull and Morrison governments, which had consistently rejected the proposal for establishing an Indigenous representative assembly in the constitution. Pinkstone identified the common ground and proposed starting a conversation about Twomey's second 2020 suggestion. Pinkstone argued that an amendment requiring the Commonwealth to make provision for Indigenous voices to be heard was consistent with the aspirations of the Uluru Statement and the stated position of the prime minister and the government. She believed it was possible to find broad support for such an amendment.

This was the kind of contribution that should have been celebrated. Pinkstone was trying to start a conversation about an amendment to the constitution that would allow the conservative government to say in good faith, "We never capitulated by agreeing to establish a new representative body in the constitution." At the same time, it would allow the Indigenous advocates to say in good faith, "We stood firm and insisted that the constitution had to oblige the Commonwealth to ensure that Indigenous voices were heard." Alas, there was increasingly little interest in finding common ground, so a suggestion like this was not welcomed. Advocates maintained that now was the time for persuading parliamentarians that they should support an amendment that established a new body in the constitution. The conservative government was content to stand by Turnbull's response to the referendum council's report. Government comments reiterated that its position had not changed, but these were sufficiently vague that Indigenous advocates could maintain that their preferred option had not been ruled out (although the government had never ruled it 'in'). People were digging in and believed that their opponents had to capitulate. There was little appetite for finding common ground.

Perhaps the last serious attempt at discussing a settlement was Andrew Bragg's *Buraadja: The liberal case for national reconciliation*, published in 2021. In this book, the Liberal senator rehearsed the history of the Liberal Party's approach to Indigenous affairs. Although the record was not perfect, he drew readers' attention to the record of achievement, and made the case for why constitutional recognition of Indigenous people was continuous with the best in the party's approach to Indigenous affairs. Bragg considered options for reform that were consistent with Liberal values, drawing inspiration from the approach taken in the Pinkstone paper. It was an attempt to meet people where they were at; to say that Liberals can have a conversation about Indigenous recognition on Liberal terms.

In 2022, the Calma-Langton report made recommendations about options for local and regional entities and a national entity. It recommended that the government first implement the local and regional entities, and that the national entity be developed out of the local and regional entities. The government accepted this recommendation and announced that Langton and Calma would chair a proposed local and regional voice establishment group, with $31.8 million committed for the process. Later that year, at the federal election on 21 May, the Labor Party achieved government and the group did not proceed as planned.

Albanese's suggestion

In his speech claiming victory on election night, Anthony Albanese's first words were to reaffirm the new government's commitment to the Uluru Statement. The symbolism of this was unmissable. It was to be a signature policy of his government. Six days later, the leaders of Australia's religious communities gathered at Barangaroo to sign a joint resolution calling for bipartisan action for a referendum. It was a significant gathering with the signing ceremony broadcast on Sky. The joint resolution was signed by the primate of the Anglican Church of Australia, the chair of the Australian Sangha Association, the grand mufti of Australia, and the presidents of the Australian Catholic Bishops Conference, National Sikh Council of Australia, Executive Council of Australian Jewry, Hindu Council of Australia, National Council of Churches in Australia, and the Uniting Church in Australia. Now that the government was explicitly committed to holding a referendum, the question was the extent to which it would listen to the religious leaders' plea to do so in a bipartisan way, and the extent to which the opposition was prepared to participate in a bipartisan process, should the government initiate one.

The new government's approach was announced in August, when the prime minister addressed the Garma festival in the northeast of Arnhem Land in the Northern Territory. He said, "Our starting point is a recommendation to add three sentences to the Constitution." This he described as an "opening bid," acknowledging, "this may not be the final form of words – but I think it's how we can get to a final form of words." He announced the three sentences that comprised the opening bid. Subsequently, the government appointed a referendum working group, to be chaired by the minister for Indigenous Australians (Linda Burney) and the special envoy for reconciliation and the implementation of the Uluru Statement from the Heart (Patrick Dodson). This was to be supported by a constitutional expert group, chaired by the attorney-general (Mark Dreyfus), which reported to the working group.

The government kept saying that it would welcome a bipartisan approach if the opposition wanted bipartisanship, but what did bipartisanship mean at this point? The government seemed to be saying, "This can be bipartisan, if you want to join us in what we're doing." To get the opposition on board, however, the government really needed to be saying something more like, "We can establish a process to find a way of doing this that works for everyone." The difficulty with the government's approach was that it chose to put forward a suggestion for an amendment to the constitution without having any public process. Bipartisanship required the recommendation for an amendment to emerge from deliberation that was independent of either the government or the opposition.

Having released the prime minister's suggestion, the government did not announce a public process to consider the suggestion before the government introduced it into the parliament. The result of these decisions was that the opposition was put in an invidious position. There was no bipartisan process for it to be part of, as there had been with the referendum council and the joint select committees when Labor was in opposition. Instead, there was a government process that would determine government policy, and the opposition could either choose to support that government policy or not once it was announced.

Conservative critique and rejection of Albanese's suggestion

In the absence of a public forum for evaluating the prime minister's Garma model and proposing alternatives, civil society stepped in. At the Sydney Institute, Gerard Henderson hosted a number of events at which people with opposing views were invited to speak. A particularly important paper was given by Louise Clegg, a member of the Sydney Bar, on 15 August. After offering a critique of the Garma model, she proceeded to offer her own alternative model for an amendment, which was a revision of the race power in section 51(xxvi) of the constitution. It was less ambitious than the Garma model. It had its own critics, both amongst constitutional lawyers who disagreed about the law, and Indigenous advocates, who felt that it did not go far enough to realise Indigenous aspirations.

The Clegg intervention was significant although it did not attract much attention. Indeed, it was significant for the fact that it did not attract attention. Here was a conservative lawyer with close ties to the right of the Liberal Party who was proposing an amendment to recognise Indigenous people in the constitution through a change to the race power. She should have been commended for having offered a conservative starting point for a conversation. What was needed was more conversations like this, in the hope of arriving at a compromise. The failure to encourage conversations like this meant that, in the end, the only conversations for conservatives to participate in were conversations about why they could not support the Garma model.

Although the government had not yet announced what form the amendment would take, on 28 November 2022, the Nationals declared that they would oppose any amendment to establish an Indigenous body in the constitution. The Liberals were yet to confirm their position. On 7 January 2023, Peter Dutton, the opposition leader, wrote a letter to the prime minister. In it, he listed fifteen questions that the opposition said people were asking but which the government had not yet answered. Advocates regarded this as a hostile tactic. The difficulty was that the government did not have answers to the questions and was not prepared to have some kind of public process to discuss them. The prospect of bipartisanship was not yet totally ruled out, but it was all but ruled out.

The situation at the time of the opening of parliament on 6 February was that advocates maintained that the Indigenous had spoken through the Uluru Statement. They saw no need for a constitutional convention to debate how the constitution should be amended. Their detractors identified a range of concerns that had not been addressed. They felt that they had not been given an opportunity to be part of an independent process that was not controlled by the government. Instead, the only process on offer had been controlled by government-appointed experts and 'elites'; a process in which they had no confidence.

Government's bill introduced and bipartisanship collapses

The government liaised with the working group in order to finalise the bill for a constitution alteration, which the attorney-general introduced into the House of Representatives on 30 March. On the same day, the bill was referred to a joint select committee of the parliament, chaired by Labor Senator Nita Green, with the Liberal MP Keith Wolahan as her deputy.

On 3 April, Julian Leeser addressed the National Press Club. Although he was the shadow minister for Indigenous Australians, the Liberals had not yet determined their position, so he was free to speak in a personal capacity. He said, "I wish the referendum was in a better place than it is," and lamented that the government was "mucking it up" by refusing to find common ground. Leeser wanted to see a referendum succeed. Given how dire the situation was, he proposed significant changes to the proposed amendment. He proposed removing the introductory language and the second of the three substantive clauses. The second clause, which dealt with the right to make representations to the parliament and the executive, he argued, raised too many questions that had not adequately been answered. He said, "I raise these issues not only at a technical level, but a political one as well. Because this clause will be the rallying point for the no campaign. For those that want the referendum to succeed, it puts the broader constitutional question at risk."

On 5 April, the Liberals announced their policy. They would oppose the government's proposal and campaign against it at a referendum. Their policy would be to have constitutional recognition of Indigenous people without enshrining a new national body in the constitution, and instead to establish local and regional bodies through legislation.

Leeser had been the shadow attorney-general and shadow minister for Indigenous Australians since the last election. The Liberal Party allowed backbenchers to dissent from party positions, but did not allow members of the shadow cabinet to advocate against party policy in the public square. Accordingly, on 11 April,

Leeser announced that he was stepping down and returning to the backbenches, so that he could exercise his right to campaign for YES in the forthcoming referendum. He was replaced as shadow attorney-general by Michaelia Cash and as shadow minister for Indigenous Australians by Jacinta Nampijinpa Price, both of whom were staunch NO advocates.

On 1 May, Sean Gordon led a delegation from Uphold & Recognise which appeared before the joint select committee to answer questions about its written submission. He had been a part of the Indigenous discussions since the Uluru Statement, was a member of the minister's working group, and had played a large part in engaging with conservatives. Gordon confirmed that he believed compromise was necessary, and that, at the very least, the reference to "executive government" could be replaced by a reference to "ministers". He could see that this was the minimum change necessary to get some people on the right of politics to campaign for YES. He told the *Sydney Morning Herald*, "The parliament has a responsibility to ensure that what we put forward is worth winning from an Indigenous perspective and from an Australian community perspective, but that it is also winnable."

On 18 May, Mick Gooda called for comprise. He said, "I've decided to speak out, and I'm sure I will be criticised because I'm beginning to be terrified we're going to lose this." Gooda's proposal was less dramatic than Leeser's but more so than Gordon's. He proposed removing the reference to the executive government, so that the new entity would be guaranteed the right to make representations to the parliament, but not to the government. He said, "I know we've compromised all our lives, but right now, we're at the pointy end, and if there needs to be a compromise to get over the line, let's do it." Although he appreciated why it was important for the new body to be able to consult with government departments and ministers, it would still be able to do this even if it was not stipulated in the constitution, which had become a major sticking point for constitutional conservatives.

Leeser, Gordon, and Gooda all supported constitutional recognition in the form of an Indigenous advisory body recognised in the constitution, but had all made the case for compromise. It was too late for compromise. The YES advocates had already nailed their colours to the mast. Their stance deprived them of any flexibility. This meant that if you did not support their preferred draft of the amendment to the constitution, you were opposed to the whole proposition of recognising Indigenous people through a constitutional guarantee that their voices would be heard in Indigenous affairs. They should not have committed to a specific draft of the amendment until there was broad enough support for that draft.

The joint select committee was given six weeks to report back to the parliament. Submissions were made in an attempt to get some kind of compromise. It was hoped that, if some concession could be extracted, this would force the opposition to rethink its position and allow a free vote for its members. This would at least have meant some members of the shadow cabinet would be free to campaign for YES. Alas, it was too late to try and find common ground. There was no appetite for compromise. The committee recommended that the bill be passed without any amendment.

Referendum campaign begins

By the time that the bill passed the House of Representatives on 31 May and the Senate on 19 June, it was clear that this was neither a bipartisan initiative nor a settlement project. The country waited for two months until, on 29 August, the prime minister announced that a referendum on the proposed law would be held on 14 October. Thus began a six-week referendum campaign. The

Referendum (Machinery Provisions) Act required the Australian Electoral Commissioner to print and distribute a pamphlet containing the official YES and NO cases written by a committee of parliamentarians who had supported and opposed the bill. Initially, the government proposed suspending this requirement, however, it relented when objections were made that it was in the public interest for the public to be properly informed of the views within the parliament. This was to be the only public funding for the campaign, as required by the referendum act. The government did allow the body running the primary YES campaign, Australians for Indigenous Constitutional Recognition to be granted tax deductibility for its Yes23 campaign. The NO campaigners did not actively seek tax deductibility for their donations, having been discouraged to do so by the government's conduct.

The Labor government's YES campaign was supported by Yes23 and other campaigns, including the Uluru Dialogue's History is Calling campaign. The Greens also campaigned for YES, after their only Indigenous member, Lidia Thorpe, split from the Greens to sit as an independent in the Senate and spearhead the Blak sovereignty movement's NO campaign. In the end there was a clear alignment between the YES case campaigners, the Labor government, and most of the progressive side of politics more generally. Perhaps not explicitly, but implicitly, they had signed up to identity politics. The gist of their argument was that all decent people should support the YES case because this Indigenous Voice is how Indigenous people said they wanted to be recognised. They had long ago rejected the idea that it was necessary to make a settlement.

The Liberal and National parties together with Advance's Fair Australia campaign prosecuted the NO Case. There were a few exceptions. Two Liberal MPs (Julian Leeser and Bridget Archer) and one senator (Andrew Bragg) campaigned for YES. They fell in behind the Liberals for Yes campaign convened by former

Australian Capital Territory chief minister Kate Carnell and Uphold & Recognise chairman Sean Gordon. This campaign sought to provide an alternative voice for YES; one that spoke the language of conservatives rather than progressives. They were joined by the Tasmanian premier, Jeremy Rockliff, and a smattering of current and former Liberal parliamentarians.

But, unsurprisingly, in the end there was a fairly clear alignment between the NO case campaigners, the opposition's Liberal and National parties, and the conservative side of politics more generally. They had explicitly or implicitly signed up to populist politics. The gist of their argument was that all 'ordinary' Australians should send a message that they will not be conned by 'the elites'. The people should instead vote NO to a proposition that, they claimed, would divide Australia by race. They never bought into the idea of a settlement because they decided that this was not really a fundamental challenge that needed to be addressed: failure, they maintained, would have repercussions for the Labor government, not for the nation.

On 14 October, YES polled 39.94% of the national vote and NO polled 60.06%. NO prevailed in every state and territory other than the Australian Capital Territory, where YES polled 61.29% of the vote. The outcome was obvious once the results started to be counted on the eastern seaboard. After voting closed in Western Australia, the Indigenous leadership who had run the YES campaign proclaimed a Week of Silence, during which no Indigenous YES campaigners would speak to the media, whilst they came to terms with what had happened.

Abandoning settlement politics fails to find common ground

Although the proposal that was put to a referendum started out as a settlement project, as the public conversation gained momentum, any real commitment to it as a settlement project dissipated. What was required was a broadening commitment to settlement politics. To be sure, there were two extremes that could never have been accommodated within a settlement.

On the one hand, there were Indigenous advocates who were never going to accept that the place of Indigenous peoples needed to be recognised in the constitution without an explicit recognition of Blak sovereignty. They were not interested in making room for people who were concerned not to disturb the way the constitution operates. They were not interested in a settlement that did not change the relationship between the Commonwealth Parliament, the Executive Government of the Commonwealth, and the High Court; one that affirmed that all Australians were treated equally by the constitution. On the other, there were those who were never going to accept that, given Indigenous peoples' history of dispossession and discrimination in Australia, it was in the national interest to create some kind of guarantee. They saw no reason why Indigenous peoples needed a guarantee that gave them reason to believe that the future would be different from the past; a guarantee that applied specifically to Indigenous people given their unique history since 1788. But more could have been done to continue the settlement project with those who were still open to it, which included the leaders of the political class – at least until well into 2022.

In this chapter's recounting of the story of the referendum, the focus has not been on explaining how the electorate engaged with the public conversation. There has not been a detailed analysis of public attitudes to the YES campaign and the NO campaign, or of the effect that these have had on the social cohesiveness of Australian society at large. Others may tell this story, but, for present purposes, it is not germane. The critical point is that the proposal was not ready for a public conversation because it did not have bipartisan support. It was not going to have bipartisan support because the proposal did not land on common ground. The focus of this chapter has been on explaining how the commitment to settlement politics broke down.

At the referendum council stage (2016-17), more should have been done to generate widespread discussion about the need to recognise Indigenous peoples in the constitution and to identify and engage seriously with the range of concerns that people had. The issues that contributed to a profound disagreement about how to recognise Indigenous peoples needed to be taken seriously at this time. It was not sufficient to focus on establishing an Indigenous consensus position. In addition to the constitutional guarantee and the extra-constitutional declaration, the council should have recommended keeping open discussion about tidying up the race provisions that mattered to certain constituencies.

After the federal election in 2022, more should have been done to generate widespread discussion about options for creating a constitutional guarantee that Indigenous voices would be heard. The prime minister should have announced a public process to consider the options and to arrive at some kind of convergence on one option. It was not sufficient for him to announce his suggestion for the drafting of an amendment at the Garma festival without this drafting having emanated out of a public process or without a commitment to initiating a public process to consider it before it became government policy. The government should have kept open discussion about the council's recommendation for a declaration as well as progressing the constitutional guarantee: the symbolic language about the three parts of Australia's identity captured the interest of some constituencies.

The prime minister was aware of the situation and failed to demonstrate the necessary leadership required by settlement politics. He was advised to find common ground and refused to act on the advice. On 9 November 2022, Frank Brennan, a highly respected Jesuit lawyer and Indigenous activist of decades' standing, wrote a letter to the prime minister imploring him to establish a parliamentary committee which would enable a "return to formal bipartisan co-operation." On 21 February 2023, more than three months later, having seen no action in this respect, he gave an interview to Ben Fordham on 2GB radio. Brennan now expressed publicly the concern that he had expressed privately and allowed 2GB to publish the letter on its website. This prompted a twelve-minute telephone call from the prime minister. Brennan reports that the prime minister was "upset" and "animated", expressing his surprise at Brennan's "political naivety" in "feeding the No case" and his "utter shock" that Brennan would choose to publish the letter. The vignette is one of a prime minister who does not want to take action to address a dire situation when warned of it. No doubt this was not an isolated incident.

Once the bill for a constitutional amendment was introduced into the parliament in 2023, more should have been done to consider how the bill could have been refined to address residual concerns and maximise support. It was not sufficient to have a six-week joint select committee that endorsed the bill without any attempt to demonstrate that concerns had been heard and addressed. The parliament should have been open to suggestions made by people like Gooda, who wanted to see this succeed, and entertained amendments to the bill that would have broadened the support base for the YES case at a referendum.

Gooda's advice was not heeded during the committee stage. At the time, he was even ridiculed publicly as a 'bedwetter'. But, with the benefit of hindsight, he was right. At each point there was a failure to maintain the bipartisanship that the government needed for this to succeed. There was a failure to acknowledge the legitimacy of disagreements about how to address the challenge of constitutional recognition, and to arrive at a solution that spoke to the range of concerns.

The challenge presented and the disagreement about how to address it were no more profound than those faced by Elizabeth I in the sixteenth century, Deakin in the first decade of the Australian federation, or Hawke and Keating in the 1980s. They were very different challenges, but they were profound in their way, as were the disagreements about how best to address them. The difference was that settlement politics prevailed. In contrast, in 2023 the referendum became a competition between advocates' identity politics and opponents' populism. Given what we know about decreasing trust and increasing polarisation in Australia, it is not surprising that the government allowed settlement politics to give way to identity politics and populist politics.

8

Restoring Settlement Politics

Politics isn't supposed to be warm and cuddly, but it doesn't have to be polarising either. Policymaking involves choices, but so does politics. Choices about politics are made by those who seek to govern, and by the governed, who choose the government in a democracy.

Settlement politics is a way of going about building political concurrence without silencing dissent. It acknowledges that people will have different approaches, but that they can converge on an outcome even if their rationale differs and their aspirations for the future differ. This was the way in which Alfred Deakin constructed the Australian Settlement in the first decade of the federation. And it was the way Bob Hawke and Paul Keating dismantled it in the 1980s with the support of John Howard.

Settlement politics has much to commend it. It promotes long-term stability if major policy decisions have the buy-in of people across the political divide. Even if they plan to implement the policies differently, there is something to be said for knowing that despite all the disagreements, there are fundamental policies that will endure despite changes in political leadership.

This book is not advancing some theoretical proposition. Settlement politics has worked in Australia in the past. It has a track record of success. Even when a specific settlement had to be abandoned, it was through settlement politics that a new way forward was forged.

Australia no longer seems to have the conditions necessary for settlement politics. Trust is decreasing and, with it, polarisation of opinion is increasing to a point at which concurrence is increasingly out of reach. This is opening up opportunities for identity politics and populist politics which are well suited to a polarised political climate.

Settlement politics is still desirable for two reasons. First, because, as a matter of first principles, it is a good way of doing politics. Secondly, because it is *our way* of doing politics: it is the way Australian politics proceeded for a century and it was the way that politics was done for two centuries before that in the English political tradition out of which the Australian political tradition grew.

It was right to embark on constitutional recognition of Indigenous peoples as a settlement project. Its failure should serve as a warning.

The 2023 referendum is a case study in the contemporary failure of settlement politics. When the proposal was being developed in the three years before the Uluru Statement from the Heart, all concerned were genuinely approaching it as a settlement project. It really was an attempt to understand a range of concerns, and to craft an approach to constitutional recognition that addressed the different concerns and that sounded compelling when explained in different political languages. Had this approach persisted, it should have been possible to achieve concurrence. It should have been possible for people who disagreed with one another to find their own ways of supporting some kind of proposal despite their differences.

Proponents gave up on the settlement project and increasingly the government and advocates of the proposal embraced identity politics as the way to craft the bill in parliament and advocate for it during the referendum campaign. This approach meant that they were increasingly deaf to the legitimate concerns of others who had not yet hardened into opponents.

Opponents, who came to include the federal opposition, settled into a populist campaign presenting the proposal as something designed in Canberra for Canberra people rather than to empower the ordinary people on the ground. They presented this as something that Indigenous elites wanted but which was opposed by ordinary Indigenous people, and which should be rejected by ordinary Australians who wanted to save the country from being divided by race.

Unsurprisingly, the inability to promote concurrence resulted in the failure to gain the necessary support on referendum day. There was no proposal that people could advocate for in a range of different ways. There was a single explicit message and an implicit message that if you did not agree with it, you were racist. It did not work and, in this instance, campaigners who espoused identity politics were defeated by those who relied on populist politics.

The result was that a referendum that was supposed to be a unifying moment instead revealed the country's division. It only confirmed that trust was declining and polarisation increasing. There was no sense in which people who approached politics differently might be able to support a proposal that was ultimately in the national interest.

This failure of settlement politics cannot be denied and it should not be ignored. It means that we are at a decisive moment in Australian political history. It is a moment at which we are faced with two options for going forward. Either we recommit ourselves to settlement politics and we work towards establishing the conditions in which this is possible, or we accept the end of settlement politics and we prepare ourselves for the consequences.

There's no going back to the past. The settlement politics of tomorrow will, no doubt, look quite different from the settlement politics of the past. It will be the settlement politics of digital natives. To arrive at this will require us to open our imaginations to new possibilities presented by the technology of tomorrow, whilst keeping at the forefront of our minds the enduring human capacities for compromise, ambiguity, and tolerance. That human beings are always capable of these means that we never need give up on settlement politics unless we choose to do so.

If we recommit to settlement politics, we need to address the declining trust and overcome entrenched division in society. There will always be disagreements, but historically it has been possible to find settlements despite disagreements. To do so, however, requires a willingness to accept that we can tolerate those who disagree with us.

If we abandon settlement politics, we need to prepare ourselves for a more hostile society in which the contrast between the fortunes of winners and losers are ever starker, and an Australia that becomes less cohesive. We shall become a society that cannot see past division.

There is a choice and we might legitimately go one way or the other. We should acknowledge the seriousness of the choice before us, however, and decide accordingly. In the 1980s, it was necessary to acknowledge the need to abandon the Australian Settlement, but this was done in a way that affirmed settlement politics. Has the time come to abandon settlement politics?

Do not go gentle into populism or identity politics.

Rage, rage against the end of settlement.

Sources

The following is not intended to be a comprehensive bibliography, but a set of references for readers who wish to follow up some of the key sources referred to in the text.

For Paul Kelly's account of the history of the 1980s, see *The End of Certainty: The story of the 1980s* (St Leonards: Allen & Unwin, 1992) and for his discussion of the 1990s, see *The March of Patriots: The struggle for Modern Australia* (Carlton: Melbourne University Press, 2009). For a critique of Kelly's approach, see Robert Manne, "Kelly Country", *The Monthly*, October 2014. Two years before Kelly published his thesis about the Australian Settlement, Gerard Henderson published his thesis about the Federation Trifecta, which provides an alternative analysis of the relationship between protectionism, arbitration, and white Australia, in the introduction to his *Australian Answers* (Milsons Point: Random House Australia, 1990). For my discussion of the Australian Settlement and its dismantling, as well other sources referred to in this section, see Damien Freeman, *Abbott's Right: The conservative tradition from Menzies to Abbott* (Carlton: Melbourne University Press, 2017). Kevin Rudd's speech at the launch of *The March of Patriots* on 7 September 2009 is available at <https://parlinfo.aph.gov.au> and Malcolm Turnbull's response in a speech on 10 September was widely reported in the media, e.g. Karlis Salna, "Turnbull fires shot in history wars", 11 September 2009: <https://news.com.au>.

Unless otherwise specified, all quotations from John Howard may be found in *A Sense of Balance* (Sydney: HarperCollins, 2022). Likewise, all quotations from Sir Roger Scruton are taken from *Our Church: A personal history of the Church of England* (London: Atlantic, 2013). For a critical review of Scruton's book, see Diarmaid MacCulloch, "Our Church by Roger Scruton – review", *The Guardian*, 19 June 2013. For a critical review of Howard's book, see Guy Rundle, "Fear and loathing in the vagueness as Howard examines Liberal ideology", 30 September 2022: <https://crikey.com.au>; and for a more measured evaluation, see Joshua Black, "John Howard calls for 'a sense of balance', but can he help the Liberal Party find it?", The Conversation, 31 August 2022.

The Edelman Trust Barometer 2023 may be accessed at <https://edelman.com.au/trust/2023/trust-barometer>. For a discussion of the relationship between trust, mistrust, and distrust in politics, see Daniel Devine, Jennifer Gaskell, Will Jennings and Gerry Stoker, "Exploring Trust, Mistrust and Distrust", Economic & Social Research Council's TrustGov Working Paper Series, 20 April 2020. For a discussion of Australian politicians' perspective on reforming democratic institutions, see Mark Evans, Gerry Stoker and Max Halupka, "How Australian Federal Politicians Would Like to Reform Their Democracy", Democracy 2025 Report No. 5. Keith Wolahan MP's maiden speech is available at <https://parlinfo.aph.gov.au>; Senator James Paterson's address to the Royal United Services Institute Victoria at <https://www.senatorpaterson.com.au>; and Andrew Hastie MP's GB News interview at <https://www.gbnews.com/news/andrew-hastie-identity-politics-arc-conference>.

For a comprehensive discussion of all the events in the referendum debate prior to the 2019 election, see Shireen Morris, *Radical Heart* (Carlton: Melbourne University Press, 2018). For the most comprehensive discussion of the YES case immediately prior to the referendum, see Megan Davis, *Voice of Reason*, Quarterly Essay 90, 2023, and for a critical yet sympathetic critique of the proposal, see the third edition of Frank Brennan, *An Indigenous Voice to Parliament: Considering a constitutional bridge* (Mulgrave: Garratt Publishing, 2023). For an analysis after the referendum, see Mick Gooda's address to the Aboriginal National Press Club, which was covered extensively in the media, including *The Australian* on 23 February 2024.

For an introduction to the Indigenous perspective on the Chancellery Group's approach, see Noel Pearson, *A Rightful Place*, Quarterly Essay 55, 2014. For the conservative perspective, see Julian Leeser's "Uphold and recognise", Greg Craven's "The law, substance and morality of recognition", and Damien Freeman and Julian Leeser's "Capturing the nation's aspirations" all in Damien Freeman and Shireen Morris (eds), *The Forgotten People: Liberal and conservative approaches to recognising indigenous peoples* (Carlton: Melbourne University Press, 2016). For the publication of the drafting suggestion, see Anne Twomey's article, "Putting words to the tune of Indigenous constitutional recognition", published on The Conversation, 20 May 2015; and her subsequent suggestions published in an article, "There are many ways to achieve Indigenous recognition in the Constitution: we must find one we can agree on", published on The Conversation on 8 July 2020.

Three papers published in the Uphold & Recognise Monograph Series are discussed in chapters 6 and 7: Warren Mundine, *Practical Recognition from the Mobs' Perspective*, Vol. 2, 2017; Murray Gleeson, *Recognition in keeping with the Constitution: A worthwhile project*, Vol. 9, 2019; and Kerry Pinkstone, *Anchoring our Commitment in the Constitution*, Vol. 10, 2020. For Louise Clegg's address to the Sydney Institute on 15 August 2022, see *The Sydney Papers Online*, Issue 58, July-September 2022; and for Julian Leeser MP's address to the National Press Club on 3 April 2023, see <https://julianleeser.com.au>. For a discussion of the joint resolution of religious leaders, see Shireen Morris and Damien Freeman, *Statements from the Soul: The moral case for the Uluru Statement from the Heart* (Collingwood: La Trobe University Press, 2023). For contrasting conservative perspectives on constitutional recognition, see the Institute of Public Affairs pamphlet, *Race Has No Place* (available at <https://ipa.org.au/race-has-no-place>); Andrew Bragg, *Buraadja: The liberal case for national reconciliation* (Redland Bay, Qld: Kapunda Press, 2021); Greg Sheridan, *Liberalism's Universal Vision Better Than a Race-Based Voice*, CIS Occasional Paper 193, November 2022; and Greg Craven and Damien Freeman, *Guaranteeing a Grassroots Megaphone: A centre-right approach to hearing Indigenous voices*, CIS Occasional Paper 195, January 2023.

EDITOR

Mao's Toe
Memoirs of the life of David Chipp—a serious correspondent

Today's Tyrants
Responding to Dyson Heydon

The Market's Morals
Responding to Jesse Norman

Tribalism's Troubles
Responding to Rowan Williams

Faith's Place
Democracy in a religious world
with Bryan Turner

Figuring Out Figurative Art
Contemporary philosophers on contemporary paintings
with Derek Matravers

The Forgotten People
Liberal and conservative approaches to recognising Indigenous peoples
with Shireen Morris

Statements from the Soul
The moral case for the Uluru Statement from the Heart
with Shireen Morris

Nonsense on Stilts
Rescuing human rights in Australia
with Catherine Renshaw

PAMPHLETEER

Radical Conservatism
Tradition as a guide for managing change

The Australian Declaration of Recognition
Capturing the nation's aspirations by recognising Indigenous Australians
with Julian Leeser

Guaranteeing a Grassroots Megaphone
A centre-right approach to hearing Indigenous voices
with Greg Craven

Amen
A history of prayers in parliament
with David Corbett

So Help Me God
A history of oaths of office
with David Corbett

Seal of Confession
The public interest in confidential communications
with Joseph Doyle

Neither Sword nor Shield
Religious freedom in principle and legislation
with Lukas Opacic

9 781923 224094